Walking with Oma

A Memoir

Angie Littlefield

NON CANADA

Publisher's note: This book is memoir. It reflects the author's present recollections of experiences over time. Some names and characteristics have been changed, some events have been compressed, and some dialogue has been recreated.

Cover design by Mary Cook. Cover colour background courtesy of Willy Fick.

Library and Archives Canada Cataloguing in Publication

Title: Walking with Oma : a memoir / Angie Littlefield.

Names: Littlefield, Angie, author.
Identifiers: Canadiana (print) 2024053476X | Canadiana (ebook) 20240534778 | ISBN 9781989689837 (softcover) | ISBN 9781989689875 (EPUB)
Subjects: LCSH: Littlefield, Angie—Family. | LCSH: Littlefield, Angie—Travel. | LCSH: Grandchildren of Holocaust survivors—Canada—Biography. | LCSH: Holocaust, Jewish (1939-1945)—Germany—Biography. | LCSH: Holocaust survivors—Germany—Biography. | LCSH: Elbe River Valley (Czech Republic and Germany)—Biography. | LCSH: Quests (Expeditions) | LCGFT: Autobiographies. | LCGFT: Biographies.

Classification: LCC DS134.42.L57 A3 2025 | DDC 940.53/18092—dc23

Printed and bound in Canada on 100% recycled paper.

Now Or Never Publishing
901, 163 Street, Surrey, British Columbia, Canada V4A 9T8

nonpublishing.com
Fighting Words.
We gratefully acknowledge the support of the Canada Council for the Arts and the British Columbia Arts Council for our publishing program.

WALKING WITH OMA

Praise for Walking with Oma

"I find your story very moving. In the final pages I was crying along with you. Not only is it moving, but also packed with colourful detail, written with a generous and honest heart. People of any heritage will understand this journey."

~Amanda Hale, author of *Mad Hatter* and *Angela of the Stones*

"*Walking with Oma* is a beautiful and moving story of one woman's desire to understand, reconstruct and come to terms with her past. In 2008, Littlefield set out on a 600-kilometres journey that her grandmother—Oma—made from Theresienstadt Concentration Camp, in the Czech Republic, back to Hamburg, Germany once the camp was liberated in 1945. But, for Littlefield, having absorbed trauma through her mother's (also a camp victim while she was pregnant) often enraged and incomprehensible behaviour, this was not only a journey into her grandmother's past, but also a personal journey of reflection and discovery in the present. On her month-long trek, replete with rain and beautiful scenery, Littlefield remembers her mother and Oma, and at the same time she questions what it is to forgive. Along with this question is the wider implied question of who it is we need to forgive. Is it our parents, who suffered, and as a result became the difficult and often incomprehensible people we knew? Or is it the wider forces that caused the horrific events? And more widely still, who do we classify as victims? Littlefield's story touches our hearts and minds as she struggles to absorb the implications of these difficult questions."

~ Ariane Blackman, author of *Learning to Leave* and *The River Doesn't Stop*

For my Moravian Ancestors

"And yet what was most troubling, if she was honest with herself, was the question her mother had raised. Her grandparents were survivors, they'd even hidden their Jewishness to survive, so what else had they been forced to do? Stella wasn't sure she wanted to know. The pain of such suffering and the price of their survival were perhaps best kept in their past. How could anyone really understand what had taken place during that dark time?"

~ Lucy E. M. Black, *Stella's Carpet*, NON Canada, 2021

Foreword

Intergenerational trauma was first described in 1966 when psychologists in Canada observed a large number of the children of Holocaust survivors seeking help at mental health clinics. Studies over the next decades showed that the transmission of trauma from one generation to the next was not unique to Holocaust survivors. It held true in many countries and cultures. Studies of the Rohinga and certain Canadian Indigenous groups demonstrated that they too had transmitted their trauma to their offspring.

I had not sought help in 1966 when I was an emaciated, nervous 19-year-old recovering from yet another serious illness—encephalitis. My mother and grandmother were Holocaust survivors and my great-grandparents had been murdered, yet those truths were not factored into our family life. We did not think in terms of Intergenerational trauma. My family's dysfunctions manifested in a distant, hostile parent and my own acting out behaviours, but, also in my illnesses, serious ones.

When I could not escape the damaging consequences of my mother's trauma, I turned her anger against myself. I had pneumonia, amenorrhoea, kidney infections, hepatitis and encephalitis before I turned 18. I was skeletal in appearance. I ceased to be ill when I broke away from my mother's influence. It took decades to realize that how I acted as a child and youth could be understood in the context of someone who had experienced the after-effects of trauma through her mother and her grandmother's, or Oma's traumatic experiences.

This memoir is the story of a journey that took me to an ancient area of the Hapsburg Empire called Moravia and 600 kilometres in the Elbe river valley in Germany in my Oma's footsteps. I went seeking my Jewish roots and reconciliation with German war guilt. What was intended to be a positive experience, all tortes with whipped cream, quickly developed a darker side. I found that the serendipity of whom I met and what I saw, forced me to walk in the footsteps of period witnesses and of my mother as well as of those of my Oma. Intergenerational trauma stared me down and I had to look deeply into myself to find what reconciliations were possible.

Chapter One: Who Am I?

"Nazi! Nazi!" the children's voices called out. They formed a solid line at the school fence. Their taunts followed me down the street. Squirrels clambered up imposing maples as the little terrors chased me home from school. The slammed wooden screen door on my uncle's house punctuated my separateness. The whole German nation's war guilt weighed upon my little shoulders. Each year when the children marched to the town cenotaph to hear about the horrific German perpetrators of WWII, I hung my head in shame. Guilty. A Nazi child.

I was baptized Lutheran in Germany after WWII and confirmed in the United Church of Canada in Ontario in the 1960s. For most of my life I thought of myself as a German-Canadian-Christian, with war guilt about the German part. Then, late in 2000 when my mother died, I inherited the family files. A quick glance showed that my grandmother, on my mother's side, who had raised my mother as Lutheran, was Jewish. Since the Jewish religion followed matrilineal descent, I wondered if I was Jewish. I wanted to look into it, but, I had no large buckets of time, not even small ones. Life was hectic and I was convinced I would never prove Jewish enough to be accepted into that community. After all, I was German-born, which carried a huge stigma.

I was an educator and a high school principal for 33 years. After I retired in 2002,. I walked 1,000 kilometres around Lake Ontario, just because I could. I became the Executive Director of a start-up art gallery in Pickering, for the challenge. I prepared two art exhibitions: one for the Holocaust Education Centre of Toronto[1] and the other for the Art Gallery of

[1] *Willy Fick: The Art of Dissent,* Lonsdale Art Gallery, 2008

Ontario.[2] The latter exhibition traveled to the Museum Ludwig in Cologne, Germany. I was busy and engaged and didn't have much time to explore Jewish roots.

What I did have was a basement of detritus after closing out my parents' home in Whitby. Finally, I began to dig into the boxes. They beckoned in the background while I worked on the exhibitions related to my paternal German relatives. My great-uncle Willy Fick and his sister Angelika Hoerle had been part of a rebellious, anti-art movement called dada, in Cologne, Germany from 1916 to 1923. I felt the time had come for me to find them recognition and thus I worked on that.

Then, in a file tabbed "Skrainka" I found documents about my mother's grandfather, Josef Skrainka, and his wife, Rosa Gruenbaum Skrainka. They were born Jewish, in Jewish houses, in the 1800s in a long ago place called Moravia in the Hapsburg Empire. Moravia later became part of the Czech Republic. I hadn't known that I had Czech roots.

I knew that my great-grandparents had died during WWII but not how, not until I used the data in the files to contact the International Tracing Service[3] in 2007. I found out that Josef Skrainka died in the Lodz Ghetto in Poland, and Rosa survived him only to be murdered shortly thereafter, most likely in a gas van at Chelmno. That was the destination for those leaving the Lodz ghetto when Rosa did. My great-grandparents were consigned to be part of the smoke that blew across Europe in 1942 and 1943.

Josef and Rosa Skrainka had smiled at me for decades from a photo on my bedroom dresser. Josef was bald, with a face that radiated confidence. Rosa was a solid, elegant woman wearing a very long strand of pearls. The photo of my great-grandparents sitting with my grandparents and my mother as little Suse

[2] *angelika hoerle: the comet of cologne dada,* Art Gallery of Ontario, 2009.

[3] The Allies created the International Tracing Service (ITS), now referred to as the Arolsen Archives, to centralize postwar efforts to locate missing persons and help survivors discover the fate of family members in the aftermath of World War II and the Holocaust.

Schilling had made me feel good about family continuity. I saw resignation, not cheer, in their slight smiles when I found out about their deaths.

I moved to a file labeled "Schilling", my mother's maiden name. It held documents about her mother, Anna Skrainka Schilling. That file included a 36-page handwritten memoir Anna penned in the 1970s titled *My Life in Music.* (Oma had studied 14 years to become a concert pianist.) My grandmother/Oma, was born in Bisenz, Moravia in 1899. She was raised in Vienna in Leopoldstadt where her parents, Josef and Rosa, lived until persecutions drove them out in 1942.

Oma was scheduled to marry the son of a Jewish industrialist in 1919. Three days before the wedding, the young man's family sent him to Switzerland. Shocking rumours circulated and the Skrainkas felt it best that Oma escape. In a posh resort on the Baltic Sea, a year later, she met a Lutheran stockbroker who proposed to look after her and the son to whom she had by then given birth—if the child was raised Lutheran.

Oma married in a civil ceremony in Hamburg on October 23, 1922. After that, for the next 21 years she lived life as the mother of two Protestant children (my mother was born in 1923), until she was betrayed as Jewish—a dire identity in Nazi Germany. In late December 1943 she received a letter to report for transport to Theresienstadt. She survived 18 months, from January 1944 to June 1945, in the concentration camp called Terezin by the Czechs. It was located just outside Prague. I knew a little about that. My Oma, was a talker and had dropped fragments of stories during our visits.

I didn't know that my mother had escaped a death march from Fuhlsbuettel Concentration Camp outside Hamburg to Kiel on the North Sea in January 1945. I first read about the death march in her restitution claim in a file tabbed *Wiedergutmachung*/restitution. My mother said in her claim that she was persecuted under the German *Nuremberg Laws* for being a *Mischling*/mixed breed, or part Jewish person. She could not go to university and she had not been able to marry her betrothed.

Most Jewish persons, and many *Mischlinge*/half-Jewish persons[4], had already been transported out of Hamburg by 1944. My mother was caught in one of the last round-ups and dragged to Fuhlsbuettel, the notorious Kolafu Concentration Camp[5] where she was imprisoned for six weeks between October and November 1944. Her father had died in 1939; her mother was in a concentration camp; her betrothed was away at war. She was alone, 21-years-old and hiding a pregnancy that made her guilty of *Rassenschande*/Disgrace of Race, a criminal offence under the *Nuremberg Laws*.

My mother was secretly betrothed to my father who was a Lutheran, a German soldier and an "Aryan". She and my father had known one another since 1939 but they could not marry. Sexual relations and marriages between Aryans and non-Aryans were prohibited.

I remembered while reading these files that during my teenage years in the 1960s my mother had once acknowledged that her mother, my Oma, was Jewish-born and that her maternal grandparents in Vienna were Jewish. But, she'd made it very clear and had emphasized the fact, that she was NOT JEWISH, and, of course, neither was I. End of story. Well, so she said.

In 2007 I found myself standing more frequently in front of the boxes, stacked like concrete blocks in our basement. My parents had thrown out nothing. What was valuable? I reached into a thick file and by chance picked out Oma's ID pass from Theresienstadt Concentration Camp, dated June 1945. I held it in my hand and stared at the image of Anna Skrainka Schilling looking downtrodden and not as I remembered her.

---

4 *Mischling*; plural: *Mischlinge* was a legal term used in Nazi Germany for persons of mixed "Aryan" and non-Aryan ancestry as they were classified by the Nuremberg racial laws of 1935. In German, the word suggests mongrel, or half-breed.

5 Fuhlsbuettel concentration camp opened in September 1933 and was known as "KolaFu". Fuhlsbuettel operated as a "police prison" from 1936; prisoners were sent from there to other concentration camps. The Fuhlsbuettel prison was part of the National-Socialist machinery of persecution.

The Oma I knew smiled, held my hand and energetically played the piano. She was always carried away in the music. If I wanted Oma audio, I just had to think of her cussing out some poor schlep. Oma was quick to take offence and someone was always doing her wrong. I chuckled as I remembered Oma's run-ins with the world. She'd frequently open with, "That man was impudent!"

The ID pass stirred more memories. Hadn't Oma mentioned she had walked almost all the way home from Theresienstadt to Hamburg after the war? Yes, the railways and transportation routes were damaged by bombing. She'd had to walk most of the way. Oma had brought out the black ankle boots with which she'd made the 1945 journey. She held them up by their laces, like trophies. The leather was polished to a high buff and the new metal heel savers gleamed in the lamp light. She insisted on putting the boots on and I saw how inappropriate the heels would have been on a long walk in a muddy river valley. I failed to ask how her boots fared through mud and rain because she had put them on and started to dance a fandango on the hardwood floor around her piano. My goodness, she was a marvel.

Oma had also told me she'd talked her way into hitching rides during that long trek home because she spoke German, Czech and passable English. I imagined my spitfire grandmother, barely 1.5 metres tall, waving her arms with excitement as she spoke with British soldiers sitting in the back of a lorry. She probably kept pushing thick black curls out of her face as the wind swept over the Elbe River and touched her. When the lorry pulled away, she was on it. Oma was a charming polyglot when she wanted to be.

The ID pass in my hands stirred something. It made me think about that 600 kilometres homeward journey Oma made in a devastated and dangerous time. It must have seemed impossible to her when she set off by herself in June 1945, and yet she did it. She had the courage.

I paused. Inchoate thoughts swirled, then took form. Could I do it? Now? Could I follow in Oma's footsteps from the Czech

Republic where my ancestors were born and walk to Hamburg where I was born? Could Oma and I go home again, together?

It was an intriguing possibility.

I retrieved Oma's boots from the basement. They were dusty, but I sat down and slipped one on. It was a tight fit. I put the other one on too and laced them up. I looked at myself in the hall mirror I'd inherited from Oma and when I did, I saw Dorothy from *The Wizard of Oz* and her magical shoes. Dorothy had had a journey ahead of her when she had on those ruby reds. Oma was telling me that I had a journey ahead of me.

I clinked together black leather heels with a puff of dust and wondered where Oma's boots would take me.

Chapter Two: The Murdering Forefather

I began research for what I tentatively thought would be a 600 kilometres walk in the Elbe River Valley. I was not yet totally certain that I would go. I also searched into my Jewish background with the information I'd found in the family files. I wanted a better understanding of where my ancestors came from and why being Jewish had either marked them for persecution or cost them their lives. I began to think more about the German, Christian, Jewish and Canadian parts of me, and I realized that the disparate parts had led different lives, for 60 years.

It had been difficult growing up in smalltown Ontario as a German child in the decade after WWII. I'd never really recovered from being taunted as a "Nazi" when I was seven-years-old. In my high school History class, the bullets on the chalk board that listed the ways in which the German nation caused WWI and WWII, felt as if they were bullets fired at me. My mother didn't help. She was negative about any Germans she met. Potential Nazis, every one. Nasty betrayers. I found it difficult even as an adult Canadian to say that I was German-born. I felt that the sins of the Nazi party hung around my neck like a placard. I wanted to take it off.

My Christian and Canadian selves were fine. Canada had provided just what my parents had sought: opportunity. I had a 33-year-career as an educator, including a ten-year stint as a high school administrator. I had married a lawyer who started his career as a Federal Prosecutor in 1981. We had a lovely daughter and two granddaughters. I had run an art gallery, written books and traveled. All was right with this world.

The Jewish part? Well, I didn't understand if I had one. Oma had written in her 36-page manuscript that she had never renounced being Jewish. My mother was adamant that she and I were not Jewish. I didn't question her. Heaven forbid if I ever went against her because there would be rage and red cheeks. Once in high school, her anger had rained down upon me after a short talk I'd had with a Guidance counsellor about routine matters. I wrote about the memory:

> *Our kitchen had painted yellow cupboards and I knew from my mother's anger-tainted red cheeks that these doors would get a workout. "How could you?" she began. I stared at her back as the door to the spice cupboard slammed shut. I saw a slight puff emit from the door as it bounced. The kitchen air now held a trace of cinnamon. "You betrayed the family! You should not have talked to that, that* witch*!" Now, she turned and glared directly at me. "What does she know? How can she know what we went through? She doesn't know suffering. You don't know suffering. How dare that teacher speak to me, to ME?" The tirade continued with the slamming of a few more yellow doors. The electric frying pan thudded onto the counter. The lid crashed upon it like a cymbal.*
>
> *The next day there was a knock on the classroom door. I was surprised to be beckoned. The Guidance counsellor waited until the classroom door closed. Then she pulled me into a close, cushioning hug. After a while, she released me, looked sympathetically into my eyes, and left. Not one word. I have long thought about that hug.*

My mother saw to it that I had no voice. She isolated our family from as many people as she could; there was no gainsaying. When she'd screamed that the teacher didn't know what she'd gone through, she should have included me. I didn't know. The impact that having a Jewish mother and Jewish grandparents had on my mother's life during the Nazi era had been profound and yet at that point in my youth, I didn't even know that her Jewish grandparents had been murdered. I had only slamming cupboards that left a hint of cinnamon in the air. I knew of nothing Jewish.

I had a great many Jewish things after 2000. I had my great-grandparents' wedding certificate and the proof of ancestry documents they were required to carry after the *Nuremberg Laws* of 1935. These provided German place names for towns where my Oma's family had lived. I had to figure out the current Czech names for these places, but, then I could find where they were. I thought to myself that I'd stroll in the towns where my Jewish ancestors lived, see beautiful landscapes, meet charming people, laugh a lot and then find a way to rid myself of the shame of Germany's dark Nazi past. Simple, right?

I kept up that improbable positive riff: I'd integrate my fractured selves; heck, I'd even find a way to bring my mother, the formidable Lady Vader, over from the dark side. After leaving home, I had emotionally distanced myself from my mother and kept away the "dark side" of my childhood experiences. Yes, a walk in the Elbe River Valley would be inquiry and therapy. The walk finally felt, well like a good idea, and almost definite.

Then, during research into the Skrainkas, the internet churned out the name of a man who had purportedly killed his Christian maidservant. The murderer was Abraham Skrainka, the same surname as that of my Jewish ancestors. That did not bode well. The corpse of Josepha Trumczmin was found in his house in 1774. The populace of Holesov in Moravia formed a mob and stormed the Jewish ghetto in retaliation for the murder of a Christian. There was a great deal of property damage but remarkably, no one was killed. I tried to find out why.

Pogroms and killing of Jews had gone hand in hand for centuries. Jews were consistently reviled as Christ-killers, usurers, infidels and drinkers of Christian blood. Blood libels, or false accusations of murder, were a constant factor in their history. Jews were thrown out of countries and empires: England in 1290, Spain in 1492, the Austrian Empire in 1670. What had happened in Holesov in 1774 to avert slaughter? More importantly, did Oma, have a murdering ancestor? Did I? The name Skrainka was rare enough for a murderer to taint our blood. Then again, perhaps, Abraham was simply a victim of a blood libel.

I started more research and then posted the information I found about Skrainkas on my website. Lucie Ondrackova, a Czech researcher, found me through the postings. She worked for Keset, a non-profit agency that documented Jewish cemeteries in the Czech Republic. She sent information about the Skrainkas and mentioned she had recently translated a book by Pinhas Yehuda Leib from Hebrew into Czech. Pinhas wrote *Sefer Nifloat/Book of Miracles* in 1774. He described the 18th century murder in Holesov from a Jewish perspective. Lucie explained the gist of the story in an email as I could not read it in Czech. I loved the charming way she showed concern about my feelings as a descendant of Skrainkas:

> *The whole story begins with a murder. A young Jewish man kills a Christian woman. She was a poor maid who was trying to earn some extra money with prostitution. And this man loved her. The whole history described in this book is fascinating. Yes, Abraham was probably the murderer, but please, don't be scared, it was not premeditated, nothing like that. It was a great tragedy for both of them. He was very young and married to another woman, but fell in love with this one, desperately.* Sefer Nifloat *literally says, that he held her with all the powers, that his* nefesh, *physical soul, had. This poor woman was said to be beautiful, but probably didn't have a very good character. Their love affair had ended badly when she tried to blackmail him and even attacked him with a knife. Abraham was known as a fiery man and things went terribly wrong from there. And, of course, it's 1774 and this is just a perfect pretext for an angry mob. So pogroms follow. But Pinhas called his book* Book of Miracles *and he means it. He called it this way, because of all the miracles that happened that led to the greatest one: During these pogroms, no one was killed. And Pinhas, who witnessed all this, was absolutely sure, it was nothing less than a miracle. Series of miracles, to be exact. Even for less pious readers than Pinhas Yehuda Leib was, it is still a pretty miraculous story, full of good people, both Christian and Jewish, who decided to stay close together in those dark times, helped each other and managed to save innocent lives.*

I loved Lucie's paraphrase and wanted to read the whole story. I also wanted to be absolutely certain there was no doubt about Abraham Skrainka as a murderer. I did not want to be guilty of my own 21st century false accusation of murder. I had Lucie's Czech version of *Sefer Nifloat* translated into English.

After I read the translation, it became clear that Abraham Skrainka was a murderer. At first I thought it could be argued that he defended himself against Josepha as she'd brandished a knife. That thought disappeared when I read that two relatives found him with Josepha in his arms. Abraham dropped Josepha to the ground and the relatives counted 42 stab wounds on her body. Blood was all over Abraham and the walls. He eventually confessed and sought to make amends with his family and his conscience.

My mother had consistently framed our family as victims. It now appeared that our family story started historically with a perpetrator. I deflated with this realization. I had fallen into complex questions about guilt on my first tentative steps towards understanding my heritage. My lawyer husband, David, came to the rescue.

"You have a good reason to visit the Czech Republic," he said. "Robbie's birthday is coming up and according to this map, the places on your family papers aren't far from Prague, a day trip. You could find Helleschau, Bisenz, Ober Becva and the other places the documents mention. Don't fixate on Abraham. He was one misdirected person. Find the other Skrainkas. They're impressive just for being land-holders in the 18th century." He paused. "You could also do that Elbe River walk you talk about. It's time."

"You mean, walk along the Elbe River, all 600 kilometres from Theresienstadt to Hamburg? Will you come?" I was tentative. I knew David had court days ahead.

"We could do the research trip in the Czech Republic, to the places connected to the Skrainkas, after Robbie's birthday party," he said and paused, "and then I'd join you about halfway through the walk in Germany."

"Halfway? You think I should walk half the trip on my own?" I asked deflated.

"Well, you could find someone else to walk the first half."

I was silenced by that challenge. How could I find someone who'd walk for three weeks along a chunk of the Elbe River? Then David unfolded a second map on the kitchen table. I saw he'd been planning. That was his way. He'd marked his part of the ancestor search in the Czech Republic with orange marker. He'd found the Czech names he thought corresponded to the German ones on my documents and circled them. He and I would go from Prague to Helleschau/Holesov and then to Ober Becva/Horni Becva and Bisenz/Bzenec before heading back to Prague. David's orange line started up again at Tangermuende in Germany and snaked towards Hamburg. The part for Person X was a thick red gash from Prague to Tangermuende.

I was excited but hid my misgivings. I didn't think I could get a Person X. I also wasn't at all certain the Moravian countryside would yield clues about the Skrainkas. I took a deep breath and switched my mind over to its usual optimism. I did have David as a travel companion for two-thirds of the way. That was good.

"Let's tell Robbie we're coming to Prague!" I blurted out. "He'll be delighted that he's the ground zero for our next big adventure."

Robbie Lavack, was our friend from North Bay. We'd met at teachers' college in Thunder Bay, Ontario 40 years before when he was flying educational programs into Indigenous communities around James Bay. Robbie could handle all types of planes because he'd flown over 80 missions for the Royal Air Force in WWII. The strapping almost two metre tall 88-year-old had visited us many times in Canada. We always laughed about our adventures in northern Ontario, such as the time he handed the dual control Cessna over to me, mid-air! The blue-eyed Canadian war hero[6] was so much part of our lives that I could not imagine the upcoming adventure without him. Robbie was currently located in

[6] LAVACK, Flight Sergeant Robert Frank [Francis] (1027207)—Distinguished Flying Medal—No.37 Squadron—awarded as per *London Gazette* dated 28 September 1943. Born in Vancouver, 1920; home there; enlisted in RAF, 1940.

Prague. It was a wonderful idea to visit, research and then launch from his place. I was excited by the possibilities ahead. Perhaps, I would find Skrainka graves. I might find traces of Oma's passage along the Elbe River. At the very least, I hoped to walk the streets and see the sights my Jewish ancestors had seen. I'd feel them around me. Something good would come of it.

Now, all I needed was that Person X and a company to move luggage to suitable daily accommodation. I was going to be 61-years-old if we started in the spring of 2008. No lugging for me.

"There's lots to do!" I said over my shoulder. "Game on!"

David laughed and bundled up his maps. Mission accomplished. He had a wonderful way to get me to go the way he knew would be best for me. The walk would do us both good.

Chapter Three: My Boon Companions

I undertook walk-related planning with the help of Augustus Tours, a bicycle trip company with headquarters in Dresden. They supplied a wonderful helper named Constanze who plotted the logistics of the 600 kilometres Elbe River valley walk. At my request, she organized period witnesses to interview along the way. I wanted to see what June 1945 in the Elbe River valley looked like through the eyes of people who had actually been there. Ten persons responded to Constanze's press release.

The departure was set for the beginning of April 2008. I looked at the daily route plans of 20 to 30 kilometres that Constanze set. My finger followed the itinerary lines along the Elbe River from page to page. It really was going to happen!

I had the plans, but no Person X. No one wanted to go. Then, Judy, a friend from teaching days, agreed. I was surprised as she had parental responsibilities for her son, and her daughter had recently married. She agreed to go from Prague to Magdeburg. There would be a gap between Magdeburg and Tangermuende but it was a short gap. I had my boon companions!

I knew Judy well. We'd shared 26-years worth of teaching experiences.[7] We had lunch daily from 1976 to 1990 when she was a Guidance and Physical Education teacher and I taught English, Drama and Art. She was caring and accommodating. We shared walks and talks in the years after I moved to other schools. We trod kilometres worth of stories through the ravines of the Greater Toronto Area. We took "walk and talk" to a totally new level after we retired in 2002.

---

[7] I had seven years of teaching experience in North Bay, Merlin and Dunnville, Ontario before I settled into Durham Region schools.

Judy and I walked all the way around Lake Ontario in 2003, roughly 1,000 kilometres. On that epic trip I discovered she was a great listener, and she didn't listen just to me. We heard tales from the poetess of Wolfe Island, from a bed and breakfast hostess who told us how the Americans won the *Battle of Sacket's Harbour* (by burning their own ships) and we collected stories from old gents who chatted in breakfast clubs on both the American and Canadian side of the border. What lives we encountered! I knew that Judy's active listening would be important on the upcoming trip. I had not shared much about my conflicted past. Judy didn't know about my experiences as a "Nazi child" or that my mother had been through the fire-bombing of Hamburg and was held in a women's prison that was also a concentration camp. I would fill her in during the walk.

Before Judy and I got underway, David and I would first celebrate Robbie's birthday and then we'd complete leg one of the journey. We'd head into the Czech hinterlands in search of my Jewish roots. The Holocaust had robbed my great-grandparents of a final resting place. Josef and Rosa Skrainka's grave marker was the photo on my dresser. I wanted to find Skrainka graves from before the Holocaust. My hope was that I could touch the past, feel connected and grieve the losses that had been denied me—just as they had been denied to millions of other families. I put a great deal of hope into the journey that David and I were about to take. There was something else as well.

Oma had died December 24, 1976, alone in her apartment and my mother on December 23, 2000 in her bed with only me beside her. Neither had come to terms with what fate handed her. Oma used tranquilizers to dull her physical and emotional pain; my mother vented like a volcano. I wanted the damaged relationships caused by trauma to stop with me. Somewhere along the way back into the past, lay the clues to healing. David would help. He was good at finding clues.

Chapter Four: We Are Butchers

Ah, what a birthday party it was! I miraculously started to sing in pidgin Czech during the festivities with Robbie's friends. I danced circles like a Dervish. With alcohol and an innate ability to mimic, the Slavic sounds spun out from me. I had to recover quickly the next morning as Robbie loaned us his car to get to the places we hoped were Skrainka heritage locations. We had to move quickly if David and I were to get to them in one day.

The GPS-led exodus through Prague's encircling thoroughfares led us into the verdant Czech countryside, rolling hills, fertile plains, and an occasional deer nibbling near the highway. It was a sunny day to enjoy, no matter what the investigative outcome. We turned onto country roads beyond Brno to arrive midday in Holesov, the place we believed to be Helleschau, the name on the documents I had along. David rested in the car while I headed into the former Jewish ghetto, once contained behind gates.

I was primed to find traces of the Skrainkas. I soaked up the streets lined with low-slung buildings and I searched windows as if the visage of Abraham Skrainka himself might shimmer through dusky panes. I wanted to find Jewish graves, maybe even that of the murdering Abraham, but the Jewish cemetery remained elusive.

I discovered the right place only when I asked directions from young people I spotted behind a hedge in a yard. The young people were propped on rakes for a rest. They were working to rehabilitate a Jewish graveyard during school holidays.Their leader offered to let me inside the ceremonial burial hall. The freshly painted, yellow, one-storey building bore a corner stone dated 1903. That was the wrong time period for the ancestors I sought, but I decided to take the opportunity to have something unlocked for me, even if it was just a building.

I saw stone relics inside, farm implements and plaques on one of which I spotted the names Simon and Adolf Skrainka. I was so excited that I ran outside to show the work detail leader my documents. While I rambled on that these Skrainkas were not necessarily related to us, the young man looked intently at the marriage record I handed him. It was of my great-grandparents Josef Skrainka and Rosa Gruenbaum, dated February 2, 1897.

"Do you want to see where Dr. Freimann, the man who married them, is buried?" he asked casually.

"Of course I do!" I pointed at the name Rabbi Jakob Freimann on the document. "He married Josef and Rosa, my great-grandparents. Is he really here?"

We walked towards Rabbi Freimann's grave. The weathered stones we passed were set into long grass that looked like faded uncombed hair. I babbled on.

"If Rabbi Freimann's here, that means I've found where the Skrainkas lived for generations. I was doubtful, you see, because the documents say Helleschau, not Holesov." I took a breath to look around the expansive red-brick-wall of the cemetery on the lowlands of the Rusava River.

"The first Jew was buried here in 1647 and the last one in 1986," my guide said as we looked at Rabbi Freimann's reverently tended grave. "You should go to the Sachova Synagogue. Freimann officiated there. On *Kristallnacht*[8] in 1938 the Nazis razed the fancy synagogue built in 1903. The plain Sachova from 1560 survived."

[8] *Kristallnacht*/The Night of Broken Glass, was a series of pogroms that took place across the Greater German Reich. Just before midnight November 9, 1938, Gestapo Chief Heinrich Mueller sent a telegram to all police units informing them that actions against Jews and their synagogues would shortly take place. The police were not to interfere unless fire threatened adjacent "Aryan" properties. In two days and nights, 1,000 synagogues were torched, 7,500 Jewish businesses looted, 30,000 Jewish males arrested and 91 Jews killed.

My guide left. I wandered through taller grasses towards the less-tended areas on the cemetery's perimeter. "My god, Skrainkas," I said out loud. I read headstones: "Zilli Bruell married Adolf, the guy from the plaque. Nocha is the wife of Gimpel. Here's Caecilie. There's Isayas." The names were like the begat of the *Bible,* yet not one Skrainka coincided with my documents. I didn't care. I felt instinctively that in this graveyard lay the anchor to the quest for my Jewish ancestors.

I tore myself away only because I wanted to experience what the Skrainkas had experienced while living, the Sachova Synagogue. I rushed to find the place where my great-grandparents Rosa and Josef had married. I was late for the wedding.

I managed to walk by the synagogue. Its apartment-like facade betrayed no religious significance. No wonder the Nazis had failed to find and destroy it. A pretty blonde warder answered my ring and I proceeded down stone steps worn by centuries of faithful footsteps to enter a high, cool, chamber outfitted with finery. I gasped. This place had to be what *kairos* meant, time out of time. The ornate scallop shells and painted floral patterns on the ceiling and walls, and the wrought iron filigree work spoke of deep religious reverence. I was in a well of faith. The synagogue had the type of reverential atmosphere a god of any religion would want to visit.

I would have liked to stay to flesh out the wedding ceremony I began to imagine for Oma's parents, Josef and Rosa. My mind had already transformed the fine, iron filigree work I saw in front of me into a wedding canopy. This *chuppah* was draped with the sheerest of cream-coloured muslin supplied by Rosa's father who my documents said dealt in textiles.

I could not tarry. This member of the wedding was due for the next leg of the journey. David's time-sensitive planning was to take us into the mountains to test if the current Horni Becva was the Ober Becva of my documents. We headed towards the Moravian-Silesian Beskydy Mountains glowing blue on the horizon.

David had enough chatter by the time I related the Skrainka discoveries of the cemetery, but I continued on to the 1897 wedding. The story included a shy Rosa clad in a fancy slim-fitting dress. It was an image I extracted from one of our family photos. David begged for mercy.

We were soon in a mountainous region through which the churlish Becva River sluiced its way to join the Morova. I scrutinized each quaint wooden house that might have been the place where the recently imagined bridegroom, Josef, was born. We drove around in the tiny village of Horni Becva, but found no clues. David turned the car towards Bzenec. I knew for sure from Oma's many documents that Bisenz was Bzenec. A pleasant-looking, middle-aged woman approached while I took photos of Saints Jan and Pavel Church, simply because I liked the look of it.

"Do you need help?" she asked tentatively as she tested her English.

"Do you know where House Number 55 Ober Becva would be?" I asked. I held out Josef's birth certificate. "My great-grandfather was born in that house."

"There," she said and pointed without hesitation. I stared at the imposing house, a street-width away from the church. The lady added, "Naturally this house is new—after World War II."

"A Jewish house beside a Christian church?" I asked.

"It was good idea, I think. In the old time House 55 was inn and butcher shop. People could refresh and—provision—I think you would say."

"A butcher shop!" I blurted out. "My great-grandfather Josef was a butcher in Vienna. I had no idea his father, Jakob, was a butcher too."

The heaven-sent historian, introduced herself as Daniela Srbova. She gently took the document from my hand. She scanned Josef Skrainka's birth certificate while I talked.

"Jakob Skrainka, his father, my word!" Daniela exclaimed.

"Does that mean something? Jakob was my great-grandfather's father."

"Go to Roznov," Daniela said and pointed back the way we'd come. I have records, back to 1700s."

I was speechless. I looked over at David, in the car, positioned forward.

"We have to go back," I said excitedly as I opened the car door.

"Why? What did that woman say? How far back?" David sputtered. He was flustered. His timing was thrown off.

"That's where my great-grandfather was born," I said and pointed at the house beside the church. "The lady back there is Daniela and she lives in Roznov. She has a Skrainka file going back to the 1700s. If the Skrainkas she's documented are ours, well, our story might begin with a butcher, not a murderer."

"And that's better?" David asked, but he turned the car to follow the lady's car. Daniela had offered to escort us. We drove to Roznov with my new pal in the lead. Daniela went for her file. The smile on her face when she returned said it all.

"He had a son, Josef, this Jakob Skrainka, born November 22, 1871, the same date as your certificate. "Yes, yes, this is your Jakob. He died in Holesov 1916. He's buried there. Lived with his daughter at the end." Daniela rifled through some old photos of the Holesov graveyard.

"Here. Nocha Skrainka's gravestone. She is your great-great grandmother."

I turned to David moved by the realization we'd succeeded. "We've found them, David. My Skrainkas."

I knew we needed to go ahead to Bzenec but I hoped we'd make it back to Holesov. I wanted to find the grave of Jakob Skrainka in Holesov. I must have missed him. I had a photo of this Jakob. He was a bearded man with a felt hat, with two young grandchildren standing by him, my Oma Anna Skrainka and her brother Robert. The photo had made him seem far away.

"They're right here," I said and looked around at the green hills that encircled us. "Our Skrainkas are here in Moravia!"

I looked back towards Daniela Srbova who placed a piece of paper in my line of sight. She moved to hand it to me and I shared it with David. The furthest back Skrainka in Jakob's line was born 1761. David made quick calculations based on the dates listed.

"Your furthest back Skrainka was 13-years-old when Josepha was murdered by Abraham."

"Okay. It's official," I laughed. "We're butchers."

"Do we still need to worry about Abraham Skrainka?" asked David.

Did we?

David and I had determined that our Skrainkas weren't directly descended from a murderer and I chose to believe that my ancestors were the citizens of Holesov who Pinhas Yehuda mentioned in *Sefer Nifloat,* those who had prevented slaughter.

"Good to go," I said, satisfied with my Skrainka roots.

The discoveries thus far had already made the journey worthwhile. What would Oma's birthplace, Bzenec, bring?

Chapter Five: The Knowledge of Lime Trees

Oma and her brother Robert were born in a speck on the Czech map. The young Skrainka family lived in Bzenec a short time, yet I wanted to feel the milieu of Oma's birthplace. The sun hung a golden drape over each tree and house as we raced against its downward motion. I spotted the first vineyards past the Hana flat lands that edged Holesov, a place that seemed eons, not hours ago. We entered rolling hills near the Slovak and Austrian borders.

"Bzenec's famous for its wines," I told David. "It's also famous for two lime trees dating to the 1100s."

"That's a bit before Oma's time," David said.

"Only one tree is left. The other split apart in 1604." I read out loud: "In 1604 there were 400 Jewish residents in 32 Jewish houses in Bzenec. They had a synagogue, hospital, and 17 smaller buildings called *Hoferi Zidoviski.* That's Jewish properties for those non-Czech speakers among us." I said this with mocking reference to my miraculous birthday-party singing in Czech.

"Anything as up-to-date as 1899 in your little book, say, when Oma was born?" David queried.

"Not really. But there is an explanation why Jews were dotted around Moravia in places as small as Horni Becva and Bzenec. In 1744, Maria Theresa, Queen of Austria and Archduchess of Hungary and Bohemia, expelled the Jews from her domains. In 1793 she let the Jews back into her Empire but she was careful to limit the population to 5,442 families. Each place in the Empire had a quota as to how many families could live there. Bzenec was restricted to only 113 Jewish families."

"Jews would have ended up on small pockets all over the empire," David reasoned. He slowed down as we entered the town of Oma's birth and then parked in the sidewalk-slab open area that was the central square of Bzenec. We looked at the prominently posted town map with no Jewish presence discernible. I approached a few passersby, but I was waved off when I attempted conversations in either English or German.

"Let's just drive around," David suggested. "You can soak up the atmosphere."

We wended our way up a vine-covered hill into an area with decoratively painted wooden doorways leading to cool, wine cellars dug into the hills. It was all very pleasant, the stenciled door drawings reminiscent of Easter egg decorations.

"Okay, if we can't find Jewish life in Bzenec," I finally said, "Let's look for that one surviving lime tree. It's 900-years-old; that has to be worth the trip to Bzenec."

We parked on the grounds of a rundown pseudo-Gothic castle, which now served as a wine company. David wanted to remain in Robbie's vehicle to rest. It was to be a long day of driving. I trotted off to look for the lime tree.

That was when I spotted a young man, woman and child. Something told me one of them spoke English. Yes! The young man understood I wished to see something *Zidoviski* or Jewish, like the cemetery or the ruins of the synagogue or some of the 17 Jewish houses in the Ghetto of Bzenec. There was a three-way debate until they finally agreed that David and I might follow them to the Jewish cemetery.

We gathered David from the car where he had nodded off. Then we strode ahead at a good clip. We passed wine stores with wooden flats of bottles ready for transport and dilapidated, two-storey stuccoed buildings in faded pastel shades, remnants of a grander Bzenec past. We started uphill through an area that had single-storey, shed-like dwellings made comely through window boxes with geraniums and flower-laden gardens. They had the same generally low structure as the Jewish houses in the Holesov ghetto. I commented to David that we were probably among the houses where my grandmother was born in 1899. David had met my ebullient Oma in Canada back in 1972. Now he looked around as if her birth home might have a plaque on it.

Further ahead, up a steep hill, I saw a well-groomed Christian cemetery replete with crosses, crucifixes, plastic flowers and etched photos of the deceased sporting their best eternal smiles. We walked on cleanly swept, paved pathways through Christian graves towards a steep slope at the back of the cemetery. Our guides pointed downhill and gestured that we were to slide down the drop-off. The Czech trio was eager to get on with the rest of their day and with hurried good-byes, our helpers were gone. David and I looked at one another. Our shoe fronts hung over the steep drop-off.

"We've come this far," I said.

"There's no other way," David said. His eyes had swept the high fence around the cemetery below us.

We slid down with whoops and minimal damage. David walked ahead as the waning light played on ancient, abandoned, head stones. We spent a long time among the dead. I saw familiar sounding names, but I could not tell how they tied to the Skrainkas. Were the midwife's hands that guided Oma into the world lying folded on moldering breasts beneath my feet? I hoped so, because that meant the good woman had been spared the hell of Theresienstadt. I knew there were men and women under the grass carpet who had known Josef and Rosa and their children Robert and Anna. I found peace knowing they made their final destiny with the grim reaper in Bzenec, not in a concentration camp. Those few Jews who had remained in Bzenec in January 1943 were deported to Theresienstadt, and from there to their deaths.

David and I retraced our steps to slab square. We lightened our mood by partaking of a gob-smacking meal replete with sausages lying in grease puddles. David insisted we drive around before we left Bzenec. We passed a simple scene near a railway station. Workmen sat at a wooden table outside a pub. They smoked and laughed over tankards of ale. The half-light transformed them into a Dutch Master painting.

We drove around some more in Bzenec. I knew David wanted me to experience the town of Oma's birth, maybe even spot the house my imagination would transform into Oma's first home. David knew it took little prompting for me to spin stories. I told him about Rosa's child-bed chamber darkened with navy flocked draperies that her father, the textile merchant, brought with him from Holesov. I always worked each little shard of information I had into bigger stories.

And thus, my imagination was off and running, picturing Oma's birth as we headed back to Prague. We were soon in the glow of lights arced over Prague, headed to share stories with Robbie. Still, I protested. The day had delivered ancestral towns and cleared the immediate family of murder, but we had not driven back through Holesov and I had not seen the 900-year-old lime tree.

"You want it all, don't you," said David with a smile.

I did. I was determined to resolve the issues of my past. There was still much to accomplish. I remembered a line from Edward Albee's play, *Zoo Story*: "Sometimes it's necessary to go a long distance out of the way to come back a short distance correctly." I had gone a long way, out of the way, to the birth places of my ancestors—hundreds of years back. The way ahead was shorter—my 61-years and 600 kilometres. I hoped to come back to Hamburg, and Canada, correctly without my childhood German war guilt.

Chapter Six: The Caper Begins

On a second day trip, David and I found the grave of my great, great-grandfather Jakob Skrainka in the Holesov Cemetery. I put my hand on the stone and tears welled up. I didn't know what it signified, but I placed a pebble on the thin headstone. Jakob and Anna Skrainka had brought ten children into the world, none of whom survived the Holocaust. I stood there with my hand on the head stone, a representative of the indomitable spirit of survival of their grandchildren and their descendants.

David and I made a third day trip to the Theresienstadt Ghetto and Museum with Robbie. Meanwhile, Daniela Srbova emailed genealogical tables, documents and photos of gravestones. She even sent a letter that my great-uncle Dr. Salomon Skrainka wrote in 1909 about the hygiene at the Roznov spa.[9] He was the spa doctor at the time Sigmund Freud's mother visited there.

David and I had done well on the first leg of the journey. I saw the beautiful lands where my ancestors lived; I had visited their graves and touched the very head stones others touched decades before me. Thanks to Daniela, I also had terrific leads to pursue for more research on Holesov, Bzenec, Horni Becva and Roznov. I could research to welcome more of my Moravian Jewish ancestors into my life.

The Czech discoveries whetted my interest to find positive connections to the German part of me. I had German friends

---

9 Rožnov (also called Bad Rosenau) became a reputable spa for "sick lungs" using warm sheep whey as a cure. People came from all over the Austria-Hungarian Empire including Sigmund Freud's mother Amalie, and Johann Gregor Mendel, the founder of genetics. A large spa park with orchestra was created and later a spa house.

who lived comfortably with their heritage and with full acknowledgment of Holocaust horror. I hoped rid myself of my childhood war guilt that had been fueled by my mother's acid drip of paranoia. I was a post-WWII child.

David departed for Canada about the same time that Judy left it. I was sad to see him go. We had already made great discoveries and had a wonderful time on our travels. Judy's flight to Prague to join me would be her first solo air adventure. One of her few international journeys had been with her family to post-WWII Germany. Her father had been a Canadian Army Quartermaster and her family was stationed in West Germany in the 1950s. I went to pick Judy up from the airport in Prague as I thought she might be agitated and she was. She had somehow exited the secure area of the airport without having her passport stamped. She was very worried about the consequences of that omission.

I diverted her in the taxi by explaining more about Robert Lavack, whom David and I called Robbie. I tried to put her at ease for their first meeting. She had heard tales about his adventurous life, but she had not had the benefit of the 40-year-friendship David and I shared with him. She might find herself overwhelmed by the boisterous storyteller.

"He won't start right away with stories about flying RAF missions in WWII, or the hang-up bomb that killed his crew, but once he starts, look out!"

I briefly imagined tall Robbie and short Oma together as I described our Canadian friend. What an unlikely pair they would have been. She survived the bombing of Hamburg; he bombed it.

"They never met, did they, Oma and Robbie?" Judy asked.

"A good thing, too," I said, laughing. "He just missed her when she was in Whitby in 1972. He was already on his way to Africa to fly for the World Health Organization's Smallpox Eradication Program."

I diverted Judy some more with the story I'd read about the house on Petrin Hill where Robbie, a retired Canadian expatriate, enjoyed life with his beagle dog, Thelma.

"Before the war, a wealthy Dr. Ruszicka lived on the main floor of the building where Robbie lives now, the whole main floor." I spread my arms as far as the taxi allowed. "Last week, Robbie took David and me to see the view from the doctor's terrace. It has a very ornate balustrade made of concrete. The splendour of this family's life was incredible, and they had a castle in Bohemia too. Their troubles started when a German military man moved into the building. The damn Nazi spied on them."

"Were the Ruszickas Jewish?" Judy asked.

"No, they weren't. The doctor's troubles began because he helped his Jewish banker. The banker was barred by Nazi occupation law from taking money out of the country. Dr. Ruszicka helped him move assets, and *that* got him sent to a concentration camp. Simply helping a Jew was enough to condemn you."

"Sent to Theresienstadt?" Judy asked.

"I'm not sure if he went there, but wherever he went, he died. His family was thrown out of this house and lost their castle..." I trailed off as we pulled up to the house.

"What happened to the Gestapo man?" Judy asked.

"Poof! He just disappeared at the end of the war."

We took our heavy bags from the taxi driver and were buzzed into the building.

"There." I pointed at engraved, polished brass. "There's the Ruszicka mail box. Their name is still on it."

We heard the welcome committee before the elevator doors opened. An eager beagle led with excited woofs, followed by Robbie, the smiling giant. The aroma of Robbie's fish cake specialty wafted in from the kitchen.We shared a lovely evening. Judy and I were beginning yet another great adventure, just like the time we had walked around Lake Ontario.

"It's cold and wet, just as it was the last time," said Judy looking out the window of Robbie's tiny balcony. We saw the lights of Prague below us. We were silent, contemplating cold, wet walking. Our last big walk, five years before, had made many memories.

"Your organizing gal called," Robbie said to break the pensive mood. He referred to Constanze of Augustus Tours. I knew from the Lake Ontario walk that day to day logistics were a big deal. I was not worried. Constanze had it in hand. We were in her company's care for 40 days, from pickup in Prague, to delivery to Theresienstadt and then on to the finale in Geesthacht on the outskirts of Hamburg. Constanze had worked out everything.

"It's an apple strudel march, really," Robbie said.

He was right. In the 60 plus years since WWII, nature and man's industry would have reclaimed the landscape through which Oma passed. We would not experience rubble, mayhem and fear. It would indeed be an apple strudel march, but I had a plan.

"I can't experience the hardships and horrors Oma faced in 1945, that's true," I said. I paused for effect before I added, "But, I am prepared to listen to hardships. I plan to interview people who were living in the Elbe River valley in 1945. Period witnesses. They'll provide a feeling for the perils Oma faced. We'll see what happened in 1945 through their eyes."

"Where will you turn up period witnesses?" Robbie asked. He was sceptical.

"I have them already," I said triumphantly. "Constanze put out a press release. We'll meet ten persons, perhaps more, who were around when Oma passed through their part of the world. Constanze's still confirming some."

"Well done," Robbie said, impressed I had this in hand.

I didn't reply because I wasn't certain it would work in the way I wanted. What if the return to the past with the period witnesses overwhelmed us? Or, if we found out nothing relevant? Bravado tended to play a large part in my planning. It had with the Lake Ontario walk. Was I on the right track now?

"Well, you'd better get a good night's rest then," Robbie said as he got up to clear the table. "Constanze's driver will be here early." He pointed us towards the guest flat at the other end of his apartment. "No need to help with the dishes," he laughed as Thelma trotted behind him ready for scraps.

It was the night before and I couldn't sleep. Judy was tucked in the far twin bed. I saw her shape under the blanket. She had the sturdy build of her Scottish ancestors. Ah, my kind friend! I looked at her lovingly. She had been the first to volunteer for

Lake Ontario and she was once again braving the unknown with me, and for me. She was a true friend.

I looked out the window where an oversized Czech flag fluttered in a chill night breeze. My mind fluttered with it. Just as before the walk around Lake Ontario I wondered: Had I bitten off more than I could chew? There was a lot beside Oma's walk home in 1945 that I had not processed. When Oma died on Christmas eve in 1976, she had been in her apartment in Hamburg sitting in an armchair. She faced a photograph of me with a letter propped against the photo. In that letter I had said, "I love you Oma, no matter what." I had penned the "no matter what" because the baby born in Bisenz/Bzenec in 1899, became a difficult adult. She was easy to anger and prone to tirades, a situation aggravated by the trauma of Theresienstadt.

My mother dusted the dust before it landed, washed and bleached dishtowels, and fretted herself into a nub weeks before her mother's visits from Germany. My mother had both her own trauma and her mother's to deal with. She had lived through an epic fire-bombing and spent terrible weeks in a women's prison, hiding her pregnancy. Thinking back to my early childhood years, there was a trauma competition between my Oma and my mother.

I remembered once in Hamburg when I spotted both Oma and my mother, silent, tense. They had tears streaming down their faces as they worked the peddles on their sewing machines that were positioned side by side in the master bedroom. Rays of light coming in from the courtyard highlighted them as if it were on a stage set. They frenetically pulled the fabric away from themselves as if the gods themselves had ordained their Sisyphean suffering and the fabric of it would never end. And, it never did.

Oma with her histrionic ways rounded out her periodic stays in Canada by sowing the seeds of discord among her children and grandchildren. She generally annoyed any relative with whom she had contact. It did not matter to me. I loved her. She was the kind touch to my face, the soft hug, the exciting piece of music.

My mother was the stick pins in the newspaper patterns she cut when she fitted the beautiful outfits she designed and sewed for me. There was a prickling danger with my mother, the fear of a tantrum—hers not mine. I did not have tantrums. I ran away, twice before I'd turned seven. I once rode the Hamburg transit system for hours shifting to sit near families. I don't remember how I made it home.

Not a surprise then that I was often placed in Oma's care as a child in Hamburg before we emigrated to Canada in 1954. There were many times when my mother could not cope. I recalled one visit to Oma's apartment when I sat in the corner of her living room with embroidery to keep me busy while she napped. I wrote up the memory because the sounds I heard that day have never left me:

> *I tried what Oma had shown but the needle from below would not go to the markings above. I pricked my stubby finger. I was sucking the cloth to reduce the blood smears when I heard a strange sound—like that of the trumpeting elephants at Hagenbeck Zoo. Was there an elephant with Oma in her bedroom?*
>
> *Suddenly, there was a huge burst, a loud "NOOOOOOO!!!!" It drew out longer than I thought possible. It wasn't like anything I knew. Staccato bursts of 'No! No! No!' followed. Abrupt silence. Whimpers.*
>
> *I recognized the whimpers. I'd heard them before. My mother whimpered. The whimpers told me what I did not want to believe. Oma had made those other sounds too. But, why? Why had she screamed? My Oma. Screaming. Why?*
>
> *After a scattering of rustles, Oma appeared at the end of the hall. I saw her as if through the wrong end of binoculars. She got bigger and smiled broadly as she brushed by to open the piano sitting in the front room with me. I held out my smudged piece-work now strangely tethered to my sleeve. Oma did not see it. She was fixated on the piano. She sorted sheet music with manic intensity. Satisfied with a selection, she sat down, nodded to a beat only she heard and used her right arm to count herself into the performance. The rapture began.*

Oma and I had exchanged visits and letters for decades after our emigration to Canada in 1954. During our last face-to-face meeting in 1972, she held our precious baby. I was lost for a long time when Oma died in 1976 with my photograph in front of her. Over the years she began to appear to me, always in the same way.

In my vision she sat quietly on a chair in a void. Around her, motes of dust traveled in shifting rays of light that originated from more than one source. Her head was bent downward. I heard and saw other figures in the background. Oma turned to speak to them in muffled tones. I made out relatives and family friends in the shifting light.They all waited. Oma turned to tell them to be patient; that I would come. I knew it was a dream when Oma talked about patience, because Oma was anything but patient. I saw that picture so many times that I could have painted it. After a while, I felt Oma was calling me with that vision. She trusted me to find the way back to her—and to the country of my birth.

I shook myself into the present, a bedroom on Petrin Hill in Prague. It was April 2008. It had taken a long time to get to this point. The next day Robbie would drive with Judy and me to see us off at Theresienstadt. We would start our walk in the footsteps of my Oma.

I tried to drift off but the sound of Oma's whimpers increased, approaching from the distance. I had written in my short piece: *But, why? Why had she screamed? My Oma. Screaming. Why?* I needed to understand more of my past.

Chapter Seven: First Steps

"Hurry, the taxi's here!" Robbie shouted at our guest-flat door.

We grabbed our bags, and rushed them down a set of stairs to the elevator that started one floor below. We saw a tiny taxi waiting outside the glass doors, on the ground floor.

Judy and I looked anxiously between our luggage and the tiny vehicle. We had taken lots of baggage since we didn't need to carry it. We were paying Constanze's company for that.

Panic evaporated when the driver masterfully sandwiched the suitcases and back packs into the trunk. That was the end of luggage worries for 40 days. The driver maneuvered through rush hour filled streets until we settled on the highway. I knew it from the trip to Theresienstadt we had taken just days before. We proceeded through flat farmland with the Sudeten mountain range glimmering to our right. We hit the picture postcard Czech Republic when we were off the main highway. I already knew the history of Theresienstadt from the recent visit.

"Our first view of the red brick garrison town built by Emperor Josef II in 1794 will be the Small Fortress." I recounted this to Judy as an experienced tour guide. "When we toured last week, the cells and the long dark tunnels reeked of torture. But, I didn't feel Oma there," I said.

"That's because the Little Fortress was a military prison, not where your Oma was kept," Robbie cut in from the front seat. "I learned things last week too. One of the photos in the visitors' centre showed the town square fenced while the Jews 'owned' the town. Hitler liked to boast he gave Theresienstadt to the Jews. They couldn't even walk on the grass. That's how much they 'owned' it."

I took over from Robbie. "I expected tears when I walked the cobbled ghetto streets where Oma survived 18 miserable months. I felt nothing. David, Robbie and I had had a quiet lunch in a restaurant overlooking the main square. I passed a ballroom on the way to the washroom. It had been beautifully restored for tourists, back to Emperor Joseph's days. I had more of a sense of Hapsburg military men dancing there, than I had of the thousands of hollow-eyed Jews who had starved to death or ended their lives suffering terrible diseases. During WWII over 33,000 men, women and children died in the town where we ate."

Now, driving a second time to Theresienstadt with Judy and Robbie, I marveled that on my first visit I had sought to find Oma's spirit there.

"Of all the places in the after-life over which a spirit could choose to hover, why would a Jew spend an iota of eternity over Theresienstadt?" I asked of no one in particular.

Robbie directed the driver past the Fortress to the Visitors' Centre. We took a flurry of photos before he left in the taxi with our driver. We shouldered our day packs and headed off towards the thick town walls. As we did, we passed the three storey high Hamburg Barracks.

"That's where Oma stayed," I said, pointing at the sign.

"Did only people from Hamburg go there?" Judy asked.

"No, that's the building's name. It was a large barracks, an entry point to the camp known as 'the sluice'. Everyone who entered the ghetto was funneled through there to strip them of any valuable items they'd brought. Valuables were collected for the Nazis. The camp had a department for sorting, disinfecting and recycling less valuable items back into the Reich."

Judy's attention had already shifted from the barracks to a dark cell in a gateway through which I saw the river glimmer. The cell suited her imagination better than a place that funneled people like water. Saturated by a sense of doom, we passed into the sunshine and bird song along the Ohre River. The weather was spring-like. White and yellow wild flowers bloomed along the edges of the fields; a game bird rose noisily from a tuft of grasses; a large rabbit bounded over chocolate-brown, newly-ploughed furrows.

We saw a granite marker near a huge spreading weeping willow when we were about 20 minutes along. Stairs led to the narrow, brown Ohre River. I stopped to translate the marker at the site.

"The Nazis dumped the ashes of 22,000 Jews from Theresienstadt into the river, here," I said and pointed. Judy and I stood at the spot where the ashes had been dispersed. I told her the ashes had previously been stored in cardboard boxes in the underground vaults of the ghetto walls. The original fortress walls were thick. The Nazis disposed of the ashes as the Russians advanced. "Got rid of the evidence," I added.

We alternately looked down at the river and up at the sky and as we did, the branches of the willow caught the light. Tiny flecks shimmered on the river. The sun had forced its way through thunderclouds. The strange light lent an El Greco appearance to the medieval town of Litomerice in the distance. A lengthy bridge and the Labe River lay ahead. We moved on.

We couldn't see the junction of the two rivers, the Ohre and the Labe. There was no grand moment when I first saw the river which wound its way from the land of my ancestors to Hamburg, the city of my birth. The Elbe River, called the Labe in the Czech Republic, refused to provide drama. We did see the castle from which the German troops fled a day before Soviet troops entered Litomerice in 1945. In my imaginings, the vision of frantic German soldiers who crisscrossed the Labe to evade capture by the Russians, blended with that of Oma walking beside the river as she started her solo journey to Hamburg in June 1945.

Judy stared at the picturesque Czech town ahead. I realized there was a huge disconnect between Theresienstadt, a walled concentration camp, and Litomerice, a scenic medieval town. I had to supply more history. I was the one who had studied in preparation for this trip.

"On May 8, 1945, when the Russian Army arrived to liberate Theresienstadt on their sweep towards Germany, the camp was crammed full with people dying of typhoid. The Nazis had driven 15,000 ill and depleted death marchers into Theresienstadt in 35 days between April 20 and May 5$^{th.}$ The death marches, and the dumping of ashes, were intended to disguise the scope of their murders in the camps the Allies liberated. Theresienstadt survivors like Oma, who'd escaped death during the deportations from Theresienstadt to Auschwitz, had to face more death, typhoid. Oma decided to leave as soon as the quarantine was lifted, and that was in June. She headed along the Ohre, as we did, and then along the Labe. She knew that the Labe turned into the Elbe and flowed all the way home." I didn't add how well-educated and well-read my Oma was. She'd finished her *Abitur* (academic school certificate) in a private girls' school in Vienna and had 14 years of music education. She knew her geography.

We walked in a beautiful spring valley while I continued to give Judy background about the Red Cross takeover and the quarantine of Theresienstadt. We had time to talk as we had to pass Litomerice to reach our day's destination. I told her about the Czech official, Imre Rosenberg,[10] who gave out passes, cash, directions and train tickets to survivors so that they could make it through the Allied occupation zones to wherever they were headed. Whereas the majority of those liberated waited for their countries to send buses to take them across Europe, stalwart individuals like Oma, who were willing to strike out on their own, left immediately after the quarantine lifted.

"Weren't most of them too weak? Or just plain afraid to head home on their own?" Judy asked.

"My Oma had a good job in the ghetto and that meant she had small quantities of food most of the time. Food rations were decided by the managers of the *Judenrat*/Jewish council and they prioritized children, youth and necessary workers. I have Oma's work record. Plus, Oma was also feisty," I said, "and she had the benefit of a good pair of leather walking shoes."

[10] Imre Rosenberg was an official of the Czech Repatriation Commission within the Social Welfare Ministry. He was responsible for 301 orphans being airlifted out of Theresienstadt to England. He eventually immigrated to Canada.

Spitting rain interchanged with sunshine until we saw our day's goal, Velke Station.

"I'm going!" Judy shouted. She bounded across rail sidings dotted with cars.

"But, we're ahead of time!" I shouted at her back. I chuckled that some things never changed. Judy had not missed one short-cut on our walk around Lake Ontario; she was not going to start on this trip. She was already back from the washroom when I arrived at the station.

"That washroom hasn't seen water since Noah," she announced with a wrinkled nose. She plunked down on the bench outside the rail station.

I looked at my watch. "Well, there's an hour before the driver picks us up. I'm going exploring." And thus started my compulsion to investigate Oma's possible overnight hiding places. Where would she have stayed in this area? She had to avoid Russian troops and panicked, fleeing German soldiers, all of them armed. I found ideal ruins as I strolled the hamlet's main street, but I concluded Oma had not stopped in Velke Station. Her first taste of freedom would have spurred her on, further than our "soft" day of 15 kilometres. Constanze was going easy on us for the first day.

I returned to Judy resting on the station bench and soon thereafter a taxi arrived. It took us back a short distance to Litomerice, and to the hotel that Constanze had arranged. We headed to our rooms noting that our bags weren't at the desk.

"There they are," said Judy as the door opened. Our bags were inside. We cleaned up, and after an exploration of the town and a lovely supper, we settled down for our first night on the road. It did not go easily.

I awoke unable to breathe. It was a panic attack. I'd had them for a decade. Once when particularly stressed by my mother, I'd had an attack while driving on a major highway. I had to use all my willpower to keep the car from lifting into the air. I knew that if I did not hold fast to the wheel that the car would leave the road and float upwards! It had felt very .real.

Now in Litomerice I recognized the signs of panic and dashed to the window. I had found that cold air and deep breaths sometimes calmed me. I flung open the casement, stuck out my head, and gulped cold, night air. Somewhat calmed, I headed to the washroom and started to sit.

"I'm on the toilet," said a disembodied voice, that had a Cheshire-cat smile, just like in *Alice in Wonderland.* I had thought Judy was in bed.

My night did not get better. I tossed and turned and watched the gauzy curtains whip in the wind. I had an overwhelming sense that Oma was in the room. I choked with emotion trying to catch her image. I wrote about that night:

> "*Oma? Oma? Are you here?" I whispered because I didn't want to wake Judy. "Oma?" I asked again. My heart pounded. Suddenly a light portal opened and I saw Oma backlit, defined by the halo of light around her. I made one microsecond of eye contact before she turned. Her back disappeared into a smoking darkness. I was totally awake at this point and marveled at what had just happened.*

"Okay, Oma," I said. "You've come to check us out. Are you staying?"

Why had I needed to ask? Oma and my mother were always with me.

Chapter Eight: Of Hounds and Snails

Judy was amazed at the long, laden, breakfast buffet. She loaded her plate and looked to pile on more.

"Cold cuts, scrambled eggs, cakes and yogurt!"

"Don't worry, 25 kilometres will walk it off," I said as I piled my plate higher. Weight gain was a constant theme for us and had been for a decade. It was a wonderful relief to be able to eat as much as we wanted.

We headed off to our start point with an unusual sense of satiety. We intended to follow the instructions in Constanze's small, spiral-bound directions book without fail, but when we saw that we were crossing a bridge, we did wonder.

"Why are we going over the river?" Judy asked.

"There's a road over there too," I pointed out. From the vantage point of the middle of the bridge, we saw that the Labe River valley had a paved bicycle path on both sides of the flood plain. Green hills rose quickly beyond the paths, a little too steep for our liking.

"We don't know which side Oma walked, so it's all the same to us," I said by way of explanation.

Judy accepted that, but she did have a bottom line. I knew that.

"As long as it's the shortest, flattest way," she emphasized.

"I told Constanze, flat and short. I warned her you'd revolt if there were hills." I was joshing her along but I secretly worried about the river's steep banks. Judy re-emphasized, "There'll be no step re-trod on my watch."

We put on our day packs and headed off in a light spitting rain that clung to our red and torquoise jackets. The rail lines kept us company in the narrow river valley. We walked at our pace of 3.5 kph, chatting as we went. The path led past colourful garden plots with sheds and diminutive houses. Excited dogs rushed to metal mesh fences to speed us along with loud barking. Most snarling canines itched to demonstrate that their bites were as bad as their barks.

"The huge white snails make calmer road companions," I said to Judy and pointed out the abundance of slimy creatures on the path with their silvery trailing.

"But they don't always make it, do they? Look at their splotched corpses," Judy said. "I wonder what draws snails from the safety of lush gardens to die in the open?"

"Maybe there is a universal force that draws things to danger," I speculated. Judy stared at me blankly. "Okay, less snail philosophy, and more talk about these gardens as a food source for Oma. By June there must have been early vegetables. What grows fast? Lettuce, radishes..." I started off the list.

"Rhubarb, peas, spinach." Judy added.

"Asparagus! Germans love asparagus," I started to say. I stopped as I saw another beast bound towards us. "Whoa, here comes another mad hound. How could Oma have squeezed a lettuce leaf by these snarlers?"

"Maybe she had an accomplice," Judy smirked.

"Well, already the plot thickens."

We engaged in banter until the village of Libochovany where we dried off in a small, ski chalet-like pub. It was warm and, as the Germans say *gemuetlich*/cosy, but for the fact the locals tossed glances at us with the speed and accuracy of knife throwers. Never mind, I thought. We will take advantage of amenities whenever we can. We had tea and I headed to the washroom.

We were not long into our 600 kilometres trek, but we already knew washrooms and restaurants were never at appropriate hunger and bladder distances. A case in point arose after several pleasant hours of marching. We hit a recreational strip not yet open for the season, a ghostly Coney Island, when Judy felt the urge.

"That's too close to the path," I told her, but she was off among trees in her well-practiced squat. I was her lookout. I spotted a figure moving around in a boat set on blocks, behind a marina, not too far away. *Policie* was marked on the boat from which a man now peered in our direction.

"Hurry up," I forced out like a ventriloquist. "There's a policeman looking at you." We dashed off with Judy zipping on the go. I looked around. Nope, no one following.

We came into scenic, wooded, mountainous terrain over the next few days. The consistent drizzle cast a lugubrious spell over the green hills. I knew the dreary look of the landscape belied our good times because the photos I studied at night in our hotels showed me that.

We enjoyed rich, plenteous fare thanks to a daily routine of walking five hours. We supped on spinach-stuffed chicken *Rouladen*, feasted on sizzling, spicy schnitzel garnished with corn, carrots and red cabbage, savoured local barley brews and relished rich, high-fat, whipped cream on all manner of tortes. The rain did not dampen the experience of great food, laughter and chatter.

The sight of the first concrete lump on the land did bring us back to Oma and her long ago ordeal.

"WWII bunker?" Judy asked as she circled a conical grey shape.

"Not necessarily," I answered. I noted that the open gun slits pointed at the river. "It could be from the split of East and West Germany at the end of WWII. The Elbe was a dividing line."

"Well you better explain how Oma survived this particular menace," Judy said as she looked between the bunker's glower and the river.

I wracked my brain for the correct history. Had the Germans created a defensive line on the east side of the Elbe before the end of the war? Did they have the time or inclination to do so? Since I could not decide, I bluffed. "I guess Oma didn't face these guns. The bunkers were built after 1945." I walked away quickly. As if I was an expert on bunkers!

"Well, it's good you're giving her safe passage," said Judy trailing behind me. "She had enough to worry about."

We picked up our pace and discussed Oma's perils a little more. The Russian Army hunted German soldiers, the locals were starving and/or angry and desperate concentration camp survivors and slave labourers were trying to get home. Everywhere there was desperation, danger and fear.

A picturesque, Renaissance castle that aroused images of princesses and ball gowns diverted us from Oma and the desperation of 1945. Shortly thereafter, we found a charming restaurant adorned with antlers of all sizes on its walls. The denizens were eager to chat with us in the warm, quaintly paneled interior. We felt welcomed into a hunting lodge and enjoyed our break among smiling men. The clouds lifted a little as we exited. Our gear was only slightly soggy.

We left remote, rustic, hill scenes and entered a more populous area. We saw scattered houses on the next bend of the path and then the bicycle path joined the road. When we stumbled upon an old train station set back from the road, we went closer to inspect its deserted grounds and the sidings behind the station.

"Raised platforms, old box cars, metal light standards..." I mused out loud because I was struck by the scene's uncanny similarity to a WWII movie set.

"Where are the guards?" Judy asked.

Judy was thinking the same thing. We both looked around for shuffling victims in striped clothes. "My mother said Oma left Hamburg for Theresienstadt on a frigid day in January in an old wooden, windowless train car," I said absentmindedly as we looked around.

"Like that one?" asked Judy pointing down the line of old cars.

We both stared at the rail car from which at any moment we expected to hear pounding and shouting. Whom would we need to rescue? Would we step up?

The sound of screeching tires from the nearby road broke the illusion.

"We still have a way to go," Judy said and urged me back to the unfriendly road. We were disappointed that we had landed on the side of the river where now a *grand prix* buzzed by us.

"Look at the road kill!" I said and pointed at flattened, desiccated frogs.

Judy looked up at the hills while I looked down. She pointed. "That path heads our way."

"Let's go!" I said. I was eager to get away from traffic of the type we had not experienced. We took a few steps through a field and joined a path, not one sanctioned by Constanze, but a path that was a relief from what had been an hour of unpleasant walking.

The sun came out when we were just up a little, away from the road. We saw green hills that flowed and overlapped. It was a bright, bucolic world. Judy, just ahead of me, looked like Julie Andrews on the poster for *The Sound of Music.* I breathed in, happy for the beauty. Alas, too soon the idyll ended as the path wended away from the river. We could not lose sight of the river. We clambered down from the heights near a small rail station. I peered into the darkness of a wooden hut attached to its back.

Oma could have sheltered in a place like that hut. All it would have taken was a friendly station master. Did Oma find kindness? There was a great deal I did not know about her way home. She had left Theresienstadt on her own but had she hidden among others? It might have been safer among groups but I'm not sure that she trusted anyone, not while on the road. I read in Oma's memoir that even in Theresienstadt she had reason for mistrust. One of the incidents she described in *My Life in Music* illustrated that mistrust. This was my translation:

> *One evening, an elderly lady from a pastor's family in Hamburg invited me to a discussion circle. She probably thought that a woman such as I, who vivaciously engaged in talk anywhere and everywhere, would make great contributions to her group. Thus it was that one evening I went along. Much to my astonishment the leader of the group was a severely crippled gentleman. The evening's theme was what we Jews should do when the scourge of Hitler was over. As was probably expected of me, I lead the conversation in a different direction. How ludicrous, I argued, to lose ourselves in "perhaps and when". We had much more pressing things to discuss.*

> *I asked what we should do to create more harmony among the Czechs, Viennese, Germans and Russian groups in the camp. I explained that there had actually been a Viennese man who stood behind me during roll call who, much to my astonishment, had brutally announced that one should string up all the Germans, meaning all the German Jews. I immediately turned around and said to him, "Well, you better start with me." He could tell from my accent that I was a German. It took all my effort to divert him from his murderous intentions and to make him understand that there were some reasonable Germans, even if Germans generally were unsympathetic to him. I said to him that I had become a German through marriage but that it had not made me what he perceived to be the usual "bad" German. I argued that it wasn't necessary to spend time illuminating the differences among Czechs, Germans and Viennese. My advice was that it was more useful to forget about the differences that made our lives difficult. They only led to contention and quarreling.*

Oma had acknowledged contention and mistrust in Theresienstadt. In June 1945 she would have known that the Elbe Valley was a place for caution. She could have been killed by Russian or German soldiers, Sudeten-Germans, slave labourers, or even the locals fearing her intentions. The longer I walked in Oma's footsteps, the more I realized that she had tremendous personal resources to undertake her solo journey. Despite what had happened to her, and could still have happened to her, she thrust herself forward into life.

Chapter Nine: Into the Fatherland

The halls of our hotel in Decin rang out with the sounds of revelers late into the night. I had earlier seen tourist buses unload at the front door of the hotel on the town's pedestrian square. "The guests are in full form now," I said looking over to Judy's bed. She was asleep. I turned back to the small laptop I used to communicate with David and Robbie. The laptop was the third person in the room. Each night I also researched the history of where we were going the next day. That night the stories I found about the borderlands between the Czech Republic and Germany kept me from sleep as much as the revelers.

We had our first encounter with a modern iteration of the Fatherland the next morning. We sat in a breakfast room full of the German party-goers from the previous night. I sent Judy to the swinging doors to the kitchen to intercept one of the silver-bellied coffee pots before the party hounds diverted even more to their tables.

"It looks as if the Germans don't have much to say this morning," I said as I looked around. I noted their cups go silently to mouths with the regularity of cuckoo clock figures. Then I turned back to Judy. "I wanted to tell you something last night, but you were already asleep."

I provided a synopsis of a story I'd read. "A long time after WWII, the Czechs kept turning up corpses of Sudeten-Germans at construction sites. They ended up storing 4,000 remains in cardboard boxes in a factory in Usti Nad Labem."

Judy stopped biting into a slice of Camembert. "We walked by abandoned factories in Usti-something-or-other yesterday, didn't we?" She was wide-eyed.

"Yes we did. The boxes with the remains were probably in one of the places we passed."

"Why?" Judy sputtered.

"Why kill so many Sudeten-Germans? Is that what you're asking?"

Judy nodded yes.

"The Sudeten-Germans cried out for Hitler to annex the Sudetenland; they welcomed him into Czechoslovakia and after the war the Czechs made them pay for that betrayal, in blood."

I watched Judy mull that over. I would tell her more about it during the day as we walked. I regularly patched information into the larger story we were building for Oma while we stepped along. We had decided early on that it was inevitable that Oma saw corpses and even murder.

Finished with breakfast and clad for a blustery day, we raised our hoods and crossed the Elbe. It was still the Labe River as we headed into the borderlands. We were not far along when a detour sign pointed uphill. We were reluctant to take the road, but our riverside path was blocked. After much exertion up a steep incline, we were parallel to the tall peaks on the far side of the river. We walked the grand and misty heights.

We passed through forests carpeted with white wildflowers and peeked into picturesque houses that hugged the hillside. The dark grey smoke that emerged from the chimneys lent something of the smell of roasting socks to the air. Wet wood I guessed.

We were underway for hours, but covered only a short distance due to the up-and-down of hills; we were soaked through several layers. When we spotted a sign, we broke Judy's cardinal rule, no extra steps. We headed upwards to the charming salon of the Hotel Piccolo. The wet clothes came off layer by layer. We placed them on various metal protuberances that stuck out of the wide open hearth of a blazing fire.

"Well there's time now for another story," I said as I gauged the steam that rose from our gear. Judy's eyes were on the menu, but she listened. I spoke softly in English as the owner's family sat nearby at the bar. Their stools edged towards our conversation.

"I read last night that just before the end of the war, a unit of the Czechoslovak Army headed into this area where we are now. The unit rounded up women, children and elderly from Postoloprty and Zatec." I placed Constanze's map over Judy's menu and used my finger to indicate the spots. "They locked most of them into a place where pheasants were kept. They herded the men into army barracks and shot 600 right away as German sympathizers. Many likely were."

That got Judy's attention.

"Three days later, the Czechs found five Sudeten teens with stolen fruit in their pockets. They lashed them 25 times, until flesh flew from their backs. That's not the worst. The Czechs marched the flayed boys into the barracks' courtyard to make their fathers watch them being shot. One dirty blonde teen survived the first salvo. He fell to his knees to beg for mercy. A Czech soldier dispatched him with a gunshot to the back of his head."

I smelled our sizzling gloves as the host family advanced as a smiling group to serve our repast. Judy watched their backs go into the kitchen before she spoke.

"Well that tops snarling dogs and bunkers. How could Oma get through here with so much hatred against Germans?"

"She was born in Czechoslovakia in a town called Bzenec, lived there as a small child. David and I visited there last week. It has a 900-year-old lime tree, not that I saw it. Anyway, Oma spoke Czech and she walked on by, just as we do."

We finished our meal quickly and escaped into the open in our warm damp clothes. It was raining and gloomy but the scenic landscape made up for the historic misdeeds that hung in the air. The hills began to show signs of the famous sandstone formations called Saxon Switzerland. From our height we had a commanding view of the Labe River valley and its craggy, eroded precipices. We watched with envy as long, low, glassed-in tourist boats floated serenely by the spectacular scenery, their passengers protected from the elements.

I faced into the rain and began to recite from *King Lear,* a play I knew well from two decades of teaching it: "Blow, winds and crack your cheeks! Rage! Blow!" I had to stop my recitation as suddenly the path, slick with rain, led steeply downwards. We were shortly back along the river.

"What do you think these patterns mean?" asked Judy as she referred to black and white designs painted on the paved path that led northward as far as we could see.

"Not a clue, but the designs are great." The diverse geometric rectangles distracted me from looking at each building as a possible border-crossing station. We would pass into Germany that day according to Constanze's instructions. We strode along the beautifully designed black and white road.

"They've reversed," I said and pulled Judy off the path to appreciate the opposing patterns. The designs had been oriented one way; now they were oriented the opposite way. "We're standing on the great divide between the Czech Republic and Germany." I looked around a landscape devoid of dwellings. "And it's a mere change in the direction of the patterns on the path!"

"There's not going to be a border booth, is there? No stamp in my passport." Judy said this a little disappointed. She was still worried about missing her passport stamp in Prague.

"Nope. No stamp. Today's border between the Czech Republic and Germany is a matter of..." I groped for a phrase. "It's a matter of 'mental orientation'."

"Well, it wasn't for those poor boys who got whipped and shot," Judy said outraged.

We didn't talk for a while. I glanced over at Judy occasionally. She could not tolerate injustice. How far would I take her into it?

Soon Judy spotted the lovely Hotel Erbgericht, our night's destination. Over its door was emblazoned the date 1720. Lots of stories in those walls. We took a short stroll through the nearby village after we cleaned up. We saw markings on houses that recorded the dates and heights of the Elbe River floods. I noted that where we stood, the water would have been over our heads in 2002 and 2006.

"All these meadow lands were under water," said Judy and pointed to the broad floodplain before us, bathed in the chiaroscuro of nightfall. "Look how far away the river is from here."

"Imagine that whole area was clogged with thousands of fleeing Sudeten-Germans. That's what Oma saw in 1945," I said. We were lost in our thoughts as the light waned.

Our next day started with new purpose. We were excited to interview our first WWII period witness. Constanze had arranged for reporter Lars Kuehl to drive us from Pirna to the home of Leonore Thielemann, a woman who could have seen Oma's passage in 1945.

Our 24 kilometres walk that day took an upward gradient towards the Lilienberg Mountain, an imposing peak around which the Elbe River routed itself. Thousands of years of water coursing by had pared little from the bold Lilienberg. Eventually the uphill path resolved itself into flatness; it was spitting only lightly. We made our way along forest paths bathed in a shade of hunter green very like the colour of the sweater my mother said Oma wore when she left for the concentration camp Theresienstadt in January 1944.

My mother had unraveled that sweater when Oma returned and kept the green wool. The same wool had made the cut in the downsizing required to emigrate to Canada in 1954. My mother had reworked it into a skirt and top for our daughter in 1975 when she was about three. I worried about the power of memory in that yarn when our little girl twirled in the joys of childhood. I still worried about what it might have done to her, all that misery in the wool.

Once when Jennifer was an infant I had raged at her for spilling a tumbler of orange juice from her high chair. I cut myself short when I recognized my rage was my mother's. I knew as an experienced educator that children did not deserve to have the heavens pulled down upon them when demonstrating developmentally appropriate actions. I stopped my tirade. My mother had not been able to stop.

Throughout my pre-teen and teen years, my bedroom shared a wall with that of my parents.I heard the tongue-lashing my father endured because of me. My mother wanted me to be severely punished for my various child and teen infractions and whenever my father did not do so, he endured her wrath. I knew the litany of misdeeds without hearing the details. My mother started to roll out my horrors before my father's shoes were off when he came home from work. A sampling of my offenses included: school books left on the dining room table; dishes not put away; contact with the girl down the street with whom I was not to associate; meals not finished; a coat not hung up; homework not started; shoes not put downstairs; sitting while she worked. I was inconsiderate, messy, mean, thoughtless, disobedient, selfish, stubborn, lazy, ungrateful… oh, so ungrateful.

I had determined early in my youth that I would never repeat my mother's disproportionate screaming. I was ashamed when in later life I had lapses. I recognized now as I walked in Judy's company beside a thick forest that I had sometimes put on my mother's trauma like Oma's green Theresienstadt sweater—thankfully it was lightly draped over my shoulders and I knew how to take it off.

Judy and I trod a spectacular, rocky route, with the river to our left and serrated sandstone cliffs to our right. Occasionally we glimpsed stretches where shepherds pastured flocks on the floodplains. There were multiples of adorable lambkins, black and white.

We easily found the editorial division of the local Pirna newspaper where our reporter-driver Lars Kuehl worked. He rushed us through ancient scenic streets to his car to get to our appointment. It was a shame to rush, as I knew from readings the night before that both Napoleon and the Italian topographical painter Canaletto had stopped there.

We rattled back the way we had just come, towards Naundorf where the 75-year-old artist Leonore Thielemann lived. She had previously charmed Lars into writing articles about her and he was interested to see how our meeting would play out. We drove up a low hill to a house surrounded by groomed flower gardens resplendent with bulbs in bloom. A buoyant redhead waited outside. I knew she was buoyant as she bounced from foot to foot with anticipation.

"Where's Frau Thielemann?" I asked. "We're looking for an elderly lady." Leonore laughed with delight and escorted us into her house.

"We will do a tour first," she said as she directed us past a table laden with treats. We proceeded through a glassed-in garden room that showed Leonore's interest in indoor flora matched her enthusiasm for colour in her outdoor world.

"My grandfather made his fortune as a gardener. He built this house," she said and waved her arms to indicate the scope of her domain. "All my life I've struggled to keep it. That was not easy in East German times."

We were now in a large living room where paintings, pastels, and sketches hung, stood on easels and were strewn on tables everywhere. It was more crowded than an art gallery.

"You surround yourself with great beauty," I said and surveyed the room.

"But you haven't seen the sketchbooks. Come, come..." And with those words trailing, she led us back to the kitchen to sample homemade chocolates, strawberries with fresh whipped cream, and champagne. She picked up a sketchbook and started to narrate stories from her travels. It was difficult to get a word in, but finally I steered the talk towards war. Lars took out his notepad.

In answer to what she remembered from 1945, Leonore started, "I think of the walking skeletons. Yes, the skeletons. I was only 13 then. I didn't know who the barely human figures could be. Later I found out the Germans were driving Buchenwald Concentration Camp prisoners past where we lived. The sight of humans treated with such brutality frightened me more than the burn victims I'd already seen."

She stopped her Buchenwald narrative to change to the firebombing of Dresden, February 13 to 15, 1945.

"We lived in Meissen during the time Dresden was bombed. The smoke stifled the skies. I saw terribly burned people come through Meissen. Pitiful. Dark faces. Covered in blankets. They had nothing." Leonore stopped. She was shaken by her memories.

I tried to get details about how Oma might have made it through the area in June 1945, but Leonore only offered, "I don't know how she could have done it. The Russians were on one side, the Americans on the other. The German soldiers fled from both. There were refugees everywhere. The Elbe valley was a violent no man's land. No rules applied." Leonore was agitated. She looked around her kitchen to steady herself and then let her narrative take a different direction.

"My father was a science professor and had a scholarly library in Dresden. It was all gone after the war. Plundered. Other people lived in our apartment. We had to move on. I remember playing on Russian tanks and getting treats from the soldiers. My mother hid. She'd heard about the Russian soldiers raping women." After another long pause and a sigh, Leonore added, "After a long time, life was more or less normal."

Leonore leafed hurriedly through more sketchbooks and then looked at her clock. She realized the evening would soon end. I marveled at Judy who had followed hours of discussions conducted exclusively in German. Judy absorbed conversations with the sheer power of her will.

Leonore accompanied us to the car. Her groomed gardens framed the last view of her. The car again sped through the rolling hills, Pirna-bound.

"I loved her paintings and her sketchbooks," said Judy. "Her plants and gardens were even better, but did you find out anything we needed for Oma?"

I sensed that the reporter Lars hung on Judy's question. I thought to myself, maybe I should reconsider the whole concept of interviewing period witnesses. Oma was 30 years older than Leonore. She was the daughter of Moravian Jews and a concentration camp survivor. Leonore was a Protestant professor's daughter who had been eight years old when the war started.

I thought about it for long time but I couldn't answer Judy's question, not yet. Leonore was younger than I'd hoped period witnesses would be. Perhaps, other witnesses would be older and would better illuminate Oma's journey.

I had nine more tries.

Chapter Ten: The Madwoman of Schlottwitz

We started the next day with a change to our pattern. We would stay in the Hotel Tulip in Dresden for three nights.

Judy shouted out excitedly, "Three nights in the same bed! Yeah! And laundry."

"Just a quick 24K and it's ours," I said as we ramped up to our 3.5 kilometre per hour stride.

We were well underway through the suburban and urban landscape between Pirna and Dresden. Villas, castles and industrial configurations replaced forests and rail corridors. I photographed the persistent presence of mistletoe. The sloppy grey dollops of the parasitic plant draped the branches of struggling trees; they did not look like the stuff of stolen kisses at Christmas. Soon the metal span of The Blue Wonder Bridge greeted us. Its steel had been painted blue immediately after it was built in 1894. It was one of the few bridges across the Elbe River that had survived WWII.

We closed in on the last leg to Dresden with little time to spare. We changed and rushed out to meet Constanze, our route planner. After some missteps, we slid into seats beside the beckoning stranger in a black leather jacket. We had agreed to meet in a movie theatre that was showing a film about WWII persecutions. The slight, dark-haired Constanze was every bit as charming as we had imagined. We followed her into a local eatery where servers in medieval garb tended to us. Constanze explained that the search for period witnesses was beyond her official duties, which involved only accommodation and luggage transfer.

"I just loved your walk and the Oma story," she enthused. "I wanted to be a part of it." She laughed nervously as if she had done something wrong, "I even went to meet Leonore!" She laughed again and added, "I loved that."

Constanze launched excitedly into details about the interviews to follow over the next two days. "You must go back the way you came," Constanze apologized. "Eva Sallweg lives in the Erzberg Mountains near the Czech border in a place called Schlottwitz. The other period witness, Siegfried Tauch, also lives back near there, but he is driving to meet you the next day here in Dresden."

"Count me out for Eva," said Judy. "I'll do laundry." I knew Judy would like this duty. It saved her the train ride back and forth over terrain already covered.

"No extra steps for me," she said. "I'll meet up with you and Siegfried the day after."

"That will be in the Café of the Frauenkirche," noted Constanze. She gave us directions on how to get there.

The next morning Judy schlepped the laundry out the door as I rushed for the first of two train connections back to Schlottwitz. Panic set in when I missed train one. My mother had drilled punctuality into me with the fear of dire consequences for tardiness. I could not figure out the public phones so that I could call to apologize for my lateness. I begged a German Rail lady to make the call.

"I couldn't make the pay phones work. Please, please, do this for me," I pleaded. I must have looked anxious, because the German Rail lady dialed and handed me the phone.

"My apologies, Frau Sallweg," I started. "I'll be on the next train, if that's all right?"

"All right then," Eva said after a pause. I sensed she was disquieted. The taxi I took from the train station in Schlottwitz pulled up to a drab complex of ten, identical, four-storey buildings: hallmarks of hasty, post-war, East German construction. Constanze had provided the correct unit number and I knocked. Eva Sallweg was pleased to see me, but she was very nervous. She repeatedly rubbed her hands on her apron.

"Keep on your shoes," she said and moved swiftly ahead.

No one kept on shoes upon entering a German home. I took mine off. Frau Sallweg led me to the living room where two people clad in dark clothing sat. I could barely make them out. The room was in shadow because the curtains were drawn. I smiled, pleased that Frau Sallweg had invited guests. I waited to be introduced. The two individuals, who turned out to be a very tall man and woman, hopped up.

"Pirna Criminal Police," they said with great weight.

"You're joking," I replied in German. I thought they were Frau Sallweg's children or friends she'd invited, and they were playing a joke on me.

"This is no joke, madam. Show us your identification," the tall male said gruffly.

They looked at me with great suspicion as I fished under my clothing for my passport. I marveled at their edginess. Did they think I might pull a gun?

"Who sent you?" the female asked with a stern, raised voice.

"Where's your accomplice?" the male added rapidly.

My head pivoted between them as they interrogated me in a brusque manner. Nothing I said allayed their suspicion. Suspicion of what?

"What's the problem, officers?" I finally asked. "I gave you my passport and the contact information for the company that arranged this interview. I phoned Frau Sallweg to say I'd be late. If Frau Sallweg was in any way worried about my visit, she could have called off the interview. She had an opportunity just an hour ago."

They continued to question me and took notes, explaining curtly that too many old people were preyed upon. Finally, I gathered my wits. I did not have to accept being treated this way. I had not wanted to come to this remote place and did so only because Frau Sallweg had volunteered. The arrangements for the interview were made through a reputable travel company. If Frau Sallweg was afraid, why had she not called off the interview when she had the opportunity? I had telephoned not an hour before!

Then it sunk in. They were convinced I was part of an extortion ring, one that robbed old folks. They had sat, waiting in the trap they set. I was their prize. I rifled through my hidden pocket and fished out one of David's business cards.

"See," I said as I laid it down with a flourish, "that's my husband's business card. You will note he is a Canadian Federal Crown Attorney, that's *Staatsanwalt.*" I paused to let it sink in.

That did it. The police left after a little more bluster about poor seniors attacked in their own homes. "She's safe," they said as they tramped off in heavy shoes they had not taken off.

Was I safe? As the door closed, I realized I had two hours with Eva before the next train. I felt suddenly murderous. Could I chat pleasantly with this woman who planned to scoop me into a police dragnet? Eva stood nervously waiting. Her cheeks beamed red, just as my mother's did when she got upset. Red-cheeked rage, how well I knew it! I took a deep breath and good sense prevailed. The least I could do after all those train rides was to get Eva's story.

"Yes, coffee and cake will be nice," I heard myself say. The hastily prepared fare Eva rattled together in the kitchen cleared the tension, a little. We chatted with a forced carnival-like tone, when Eva's son arrived in a sweat. With the anxiety she'd churned up about murdering female thugs, Eva's son had run to her flat on a work break to make sure his mother was still alive. He returned to work once he was reassured I was not a robber. Eva started to tell her story.

"I was nine years old on February 13th when the sirens sounded and the radio warned of bombers." My mind drifted immediately to Leonore Thielemann at Naundorf. Eva was an even younger child witness than her!

"We didn't have a shelter so we headed to the Palais basement. I stopped to stare at the strange Christmas tree lights in the sky, and mother practically ripped my arm off." Eva looked directly at me and rubbed her left arm as if I'd pulled it. Satisfied that we were still a couch apart, she continued.

"We made it inside as the first bombs fell. The smaller children began to cry. Then the light went out. Someone lit two candles. In that half-light the sounds of the bombs became louder, closer. The ground and walls shook. The emergency exit wall collapsed right where I sat. 'Remain calm!' cried our air raid warden, Herr Otto. Women rushed their children out of harm's way and then clambered to clear the emergency exit. Who else was going to do it?"

Eva, with large, child-like eyes, stopped to look at me for the answer.

"When the bombs seemed lighter, we left. I was shocked by what I saw. The windows of the Hygiene Museum were gone, glass everywhere, all around us a sea of flames. The wind lifted up people around us and sucked them into the flames." Eva fluttered her arms in a bizarre dumb show and then let them plummet to her lap.

"What else?" I prompted.

"In large gardens, the treetops burned. I saw people jump into fountains. At first there were horrific screams from the fountains and then it became deadly still." Eva looked at me, "The people boiled to death, you know that?" Eva waited for that to sink in with the same horror it had for a nine-year-old in 1945.

"Yes, I know. Horrible," I said. "I read about those who jumped into canals during the firebombing of Hamburg in 1943. Humans boiled to death amid flames on the water. Horrible."

"Yes, and still the bombs kept exploding," Eva continued, "and still more people were pulled into the heart of the flames. They flew past me—"

The arrival of a lady who appeared in the doorway to the living room cut Eva off. The lady was of Eva's vintage and out of breath as she'd driven in a frenzy from Dresden. Although Eva assured her that the Pirna Criminal Police and her son had cleared me, the newcomer remained suspiciously alert, as if Judy might be lurking behind the curtains with a machete, and that was why we'd been talking nicely.

I kept willing my watch to move faster. Finally, Eva and her suspicious friend walked me to the train station. At the transfer point I made the platform changes, but didn't manage to cancel my ticket.

"Your ticket, madam," the conductor said peremptorily, with her hand out. I wondered why she selected me. She had passed the other commuters without a glance. Someone dressed in dark clothes lurked behind her. Maybe a trainee?

"I didn't have time to devalue it," I began in German. When she still stared, I added in English, "It's my first time on this train. I'm not from here."

She stared at my ticket; the commuters stared at the floor; tense seconds ticked by. Finally she shrugged her shoulders, devalued the ticket, let out a deflating hiss and left me with the gentleman in dark clothes who now appeared in the space she had vacated.

"Security Police," the man said as he flashed something in a leather etui. "Your passport."

I produced the document for the second time that day. The dark-clad one spent what seemed hours to pore over it. I heard the pages turn in the quiet of the car. Finally, he was done. Neither he, nor the conductor, had glanced at anyone else.

It was the second time that day I had allowed dark-suited people carrying an air of officialdom to intimidate me. How little it took to become compliant. How silently everyone watched. It helped me to imagine the days of Nazi fear-mongering through which my mother and Oma had lived.

"I don't know where to begin," I spewed forth in our room at the Hotel Tulip. "I spent an afternoon with a crazy lady, and was twice, yes twice, questioned by officials."

Judy took one look at me and knew I was not ready to admire the laundry stacked in neat piles behind her.

"If I had not gotten such a good story, I'd be even more upset," I said and collapsed on the bed.

"Eva has a good story?" Judy asked. She prompted me just a little with her tone.

"Yes, she did. Her memories of the fire-bombing were incredible, and her experiences afterwards helped me picture Oma moving through this area. But—"

Judy cut me off. "Tell me what you remember."

I told Judy about the fire-bombing and how after that Eva started into what happened when the farmers came to collect the refugees. She'd seen people like Oma move through their area in June.

"She told the same story that's in Kurt Vonnegut's *Slaughter House Nine.* How prisoners from the Koenigstein Fortress brought thousands of corpses to Alt Markt. The prisoners built wooden piles on which the bodies were incinerated. Their ashes are under the city square where you and I stood yesterday." The ghosts of the past reached up towards us from the very ground on which we trod.

"I think the square is near where we're meeting Siegfried Tauch tomorrow," Judy said to break the spell. "Now, tell me about the police."

"First, the successes of the laundry," I said pointing to the freshly folded clothing. "Let the present at this moment triumph over the past."

"If it can," said Judy, smiling at her day's handiwork.

With the stories of the Pirna criminal police and the security police on the train yet to come, I wondered: Could the present triumph over the past?

That night Frau Sallweg's red cheeks flashed before me. I characterized her as "mad". She was, but, it was a paranoia induced by trauma. Both Eva and my mother had gone through horrific days of fire-bombing, my mother in Hamburg in 1943 and Eva in Dresden in 1945. My mother never said a word about it; Eva called forth chilling details 63 years afterwards. I hadn't told Judy the gruesome details Eva shared: the body parts hanging on trolley wires; a human being fused with a gate. Eva saw this when she was *nine!* Allied soldiers liberating concentration camps and Holocaust survivors saw different but equally unsettling horrors. They simply saw too much and it stayed with them.

I had dismissed Eva as "The Madwoman of Schlottwitz", but through her I began to appreciate the skeins of war that unwound into the present. When Holocaust survivors, WWII soldiers and child witnesses like Eva became parents, trauma had offspring.

Chapter Eleven: We Were All Hamsters Then

We had a morning date with ashes. Well, really with period witness Siegfried Tauch. He was to meet us at the Café of the Frauenkirche near the area where the ashes of Dresden's dead lay under the city. Judy and I were early, yet Siegfried already sat upstairs drinking inky black coffee from a fine china cup. He had driven from his home that was a mere nine kilometres from the Czech border. What was a walk of several days for Judy and me was an hour's drive for him. As I waved at the solid-looking retired steelworker with a silver brush cut, I whispered to Judy, "He looks a lot calmer than crazy you-know-who." I was still shaken by Eva Sallweg's paranoia. Like my mother, she saw evil behind everything.

"And we don't need to go backwards," Judy whispered.

The 72-year-old sitting before us was nine in 1945, just as Eva had been. Judy and I were racking up a third child witness. He spoke excellent English. With the niceties out of the way, Siegfried took out his map of 1928 Dresden. He had volunteered to be a period witness and he was eager to perform.

"This is where I lived on Fisch Platz," he said as he pointed proudly. "The square isn't there now; it was destroyed by bombing. They didn't rebuild it. Most people don't realize we lost streets in the inner core. Many of the places I remember as a child, like," Siegfried pointed again at the map. "Here was the store where my mother went to buy socks. All gone."

Siegfried paused to take a sip of coffee. Very quickly another story filled his mind. As with Eva, the narrative poured forth in an excited stream.

"We'd been spared bombings up to February 1945. I was in the hospital in 1942 with appendicitis, when a single bomb hit a wedding party.That was it for Dresden. The war appeared to be coming to an end and then bam!" Siegfried said raising his hands. "The sirens and bombs on February 13th sent our neighbours to the shelter in the Post Office. My mother and I went to the basement of our home at Fisch Platz. When we left the basement shelter, nothing, I mean nothing was standing. As far as the eye could see, the area was flat." Siegfried made a gesture with both beefy hands to indicate a straight line.

Siegfried and Eva were child witnesses to the three day Allied attack on Dresden from February 13 to 15, 1945 when the war was winding down. The 800-bomber raid that dropped 2,700 tons of explosives and incendiaries was retaliatory. It came three weeks after the horrors of the Auschwitz Concentration Camp greeted the liberators and as an answer to Hitler's last ditch offensive, *The Battle of the Bulge.*

Siegfried described how he and his mother had headed out of the city. In Alt Markt, where Eva had said the corpses were later burned, the statue of proud *Germania*, stood among pock-marked cement and ruins. The Post Office where his neighbours had sheltered was in ruins.

"Were they alive?" Siegfried asked rhetorically about his neighbours. He and his mother joined the people trudging along. He added, "We were all refugees as we moved into the country."

Siegfried paused, relieved once again in memory to leave the devastated city. Judy, who had not heard such things first-hand, jumped in.

"You lost everything? There was nothing left at Fisch Platz?" she asked.

"Corpses." Siegfried said. He used the word "corpses" with force to cut off further inquiry. "Mother and I headed off in the midst of the columns of refugees and soldiers moving along the river. When we made it to Freital, a small place southwest of Dresden, we stayed there for the next three to four years. People took in strangers. They had to."

"I'm interested in June," I said. "I think my Oma passed the Freital area then."

"By June, well, I can tell you we were all hungry in June 1945. The Elbe valley was filled with refugees. The farmers wanted something in trade you know. We had nothing. So we went into the fields. I scrambled over furrows looking for wheat or potato remnants, scooped them into my pockets. I ran as fast as I could whenever a lookout screamed 'Farmer!' "

"And Oma?" Judy prompted.

"People like your Oma, they took from the fields too. We were all hamsters, then. That's how we survived. I can tell you for sure that your Oma would have had dirt under her fingernails. That summer, there were slim pickings anywhere in the vicinity of Dresden. So many hungry, so many on the road, so many..."

Siegfried stopped; he was done. He inspected his workman's hands still before us as if tagged for evidence on the table. We were all silent, lost in his images.

All of a sudden two ladies appeared. "Ready for your pictures?" a fresh-faced reporter asked. Constanze had arranged for reporters and photographers to meet us and two now presented themselves at our table in the café.

"*Jawohl*!" replied Siegfried with enthusiasm as if waiting for this very moment. It was cool and windy, but there was sunshine as the photographers snapped away. Siegfried and Judy enjoyed themselves, posing and chatting away.

"I can see how Siegfried made a success in life," said Judy as he walked away across the Frauenkirche Square. "He takes everything in stride."

"He's a breath of fresh air," I said.

"You mean after Eva?" Judy asked.

"Well, let's just say, it's a nice way to end our stay in Dresden."

We had enjoyed our three nights in the facsimile city of Dresden, one totally rebuilt after the war. There was a newness to it. How much easier it had been to rebuild a city than it was for trauma victims to rebuild their lives. I thought of Dresden's

New Synagogue, completed in 2001. It was built on the same location as the Semper Synagogue destroyed in 1938 on *Kristallnacht.* It looked like a fortress. I was worried that the architecture reflected a Jewish community traumatized and unable to trust. Then I saw a black-clad teacher with a group of black-clad young Jewish lads, laughing as they exited the New Synagogue. The architecture was severe, but, I sensed that with subsequent generations, lives were being rebuilt.

The next day we walked on wide flood plains and I felt the weight of Siegfried's narrative. After all, he'd been a child when the bombs wiped out the life he'd known. He had not been in the Hitler Youth Group; neither he nor his mother had been part of the Nazi mechanism of evil. And yet, they lost all. Leonore, Eva and Siegfried were children when they were caught up in the Nazi party's evil.

Judy and I were headed to Meissen, the place where Leonore Thielemann had seen Buchenwald Concentration Camp survivors on a death march. The beautiful German landscape we passed was haunted by their shadowy walking corpses. The slight wind carried whispers from the river.

Colourful flowers diverted my dark thoughts to gardening when we made it to a particularly beautiful series of allotment gardens along the river. I had a beautiful yard at home in Toronto where bloodroot, hellebore, scilla and winter aconite bloomed in early spring. I loved gardens and I took the opportunity to reminisce about the post-WWII years when my family had a garden plot outside Hamburg. Maybe that was where I had developed my love of plants.

"There was this small shed, like the ones we're seeing," I said pointing one out to Judy, "where I spent a nap or two. My brother told me recently he remembered the rain barrel and the prickly elderberry bush. My parents grew vegetables in the hungry years from 1945 into the early 50s." I turned to Judy to indicate bushes. "But, my parents' real loves were currant and gooseberry bushes. I still see my father perched on a tiny wooden stool patiently plucking each berry as if it were going into a ledger. He was an accountant, you know; careful counting came naturally to him. My mother made something called *Rote Grueze*, a red pudding set with gelatin. I was too young to understand how gelatin worked. I thought my mother could make liquid congeal. I watched the magic take place on the wood-burning stove in the kitchen as she stirred and sang to the redness in the pot." Strange how I frequently thought of my mother in witches' terms. I laughed to myself. Nope, no trauma here.

We continued to walk past gardens until a small place called Coswig. There we politely asked a man if there was a café nearby. He was dumbfounded. He stuttered over what he should tell us and dropped back. Suddenly the direction-giver was beside us on his bicycle when we had gone a few paces along the path, now ready to impart precise directions. When we were at the café, Judy said, "Odd, isn't it. Once the surprise of first contact is over, everyone is ready to help, but we sure do get strange looks just for asking."

"Germans live by the saying, 'Don't talk to strangers,'" I said. "Well, my mother did. She trusted no one." I told Judy about a German family that lived up the street from us in Whitby in the 1960s. They had five children doing well in school and I thought that my mother would be pleased to have me play with the girls.

"She'd screamed 'NO!' as if I'd suggested coffee and cake with Hitler." I explained my mother's loud reaction to Judy. My mother, upon meeting this German mother on the street, had managed to work a query into a casual conversation, only to be horrified by the answer.

"They came to Canada in 1947. 1947! *Only Nazis got out of Germany that fast!*" My mother had shouted that at me as if I surely understood the significance of 1947. I hadn't. I did, however, know enough to distance myself from German children or suffer the consequences of my mother's wrath.

The bakery-café the stranger recommended was wonderful, laden with pastries and freshly baked breads in all shades of sandy beige to dusky brown. A pleasant yeasty aroma wafted around us. The proprietress apologized for not having a public washroom. She rushed to get a cloth to wash Judy's hands. She washed mine too. We were cleansed in a pastry shrine! It felt as if we'd been anointed by the holy oil of bread-making.

Back by the river, we plodded on. Our role on this adventure was to walk, and walk we did. My feet bore the evidence. I sported frightful blisters on each heel. Oma had never mentioned blisters, but then, she had carried the deeper pain of 18 months in Theresienstadt with her. I knew from her memoir that she had lost friends in the camp. She described the handicapped discussion leader who had asked her to work with him in the Department of Social Hygiene, a friend she lost:

> *Mr. Braun's work involved the sick and dying whom we tended in the ways that ordinary life had taught us. I took on the task of helping the dying. I tried to minister to them in a simple motherly fashion. When one of them looked at me with gratitude, I knew I had found the right way to ease the path towards death.*
>
> *In the meantime, Mr. Braun read or sang to those who were less seriously ill. Sometimes he told them stories or his thoughts on a suitable theme. We would discuss these conversations ahead of time and I would write down speaking points for him so that he could fluidly advance his talk with his patients. Since his legs were 95% crippled, I was his 'head' and his 'feet'. I say that, but in fact, Mr Braun could use his head very well and his hands. It was his body that had become shrunken. I could carry him in my outstretched hands to wash him in a basin! At his wheelchair, psychically damaged individuals stood still hoping to absorb peace and find consolation. He was a remarkable man and even today my mood lifts when I think of him. Mr Braun perished in the second to last transport to Auschwitz.*

Oma described other losses in the memoir and she lost even more beloved relatives and friends than she described in writing. She had borne the pain and losses silently.

Hills grew out of the flat areas as I proceeded painfully towards Meissen. The gentle slopes indicated the beginning of the Elbe's wine lands. We saw stately homes that had witnessed generations of vintners thrive on their stock. I fixated on getting to Meissen ignoring the splendours of the historic buildings, quaint wine taverns and fruitful hillsides of the Saxon Wine Route. It had been a longer day than any we had undertaken so far and my feet knew it.

Soon enough, the imposing citadel of Meissen rose majestically into view. It was stunning. The castle and cathedral overlapped one another high up on a sheer rock face; medieval houses clustered below. We crossed the river and made our way through pleasant residential streets until we found our hotel, a former villa that sat on the river's edge. We swung open the windows of our room and took pictures across the Elbe.

We had begun our day over the ashes of Dresden; we ended it with the Elbe singing below our windows in Meissen. Daily the natural beauties of the walk and the camaraderie of our time together jostled with the memories of the past that period witnesses stirred. I held past and present balanced on an emotional weigh scale.

Chapter Twelve: The Lieutenant with a Purse

Our daily routine at this point was to clean up and explore the end-of-the-day destination. I wanted to see ancient Meissen of porcelain fame, but once my running shoes were off I saw my heels were in horrific shape.

"If you can hobble, head to the cobble," Judy said jokingly.

I put on a brave front. "I don't mind a little endeavour. We can do brunch and check out Meissen porcelain." I gingerly put on another of the blister pads I had along.

"The porcelain part won't be hard," Judy said. "Every second store window on the way into town displayed porcelain, modern and antique."

I walked with a carefully controlled gait until we spotted the Meissen City Hall Restaurant; it was by far the oldest eatery in town. Like many things at this point in the journey, it reminded me of a story.

"My father worked for the restaurant *Ratsweinkeller* under the city hall in Hamburg," I explained. "It's made me partial to dark enclaves. My brother bowed and I performed exquisite curtsies for his co-workers whenever we visited him at work. I believe there was applause involved." Judy found that hard to believe.

"I think we should have worn chain mail," she said as she looked around while the waiter toured us through connected chambers with low Romanesque vaulted ceilings.

We enjoyed a lovely *Bratwurst* served to the sound of the Beatles. I limped around more of scenic Meissen afterward. I tried my best to appreciate the Gothic architecture, meandering cobbled streets, traditional gabled houses and the tall tower of Albrechtsburg Castle. Charm, charm, charm.

"This is a spectacular little town, probably what most people picture if they think of old villages along Germany's big rivers," I said.

"Well, we're scheduled to leave this beauty tomorrow and judging by your gait that's a challenge," Judy said. She was right.

Back at the villa-hotel, while I dealt with blisters on blisters, Judy fretted. She'd noticed her luggage handle was broken. She kept fiddling with the handle but I knew her well. She wasn't merely fiddling with a damaged bag. She was troubled about something. She wanted to talk it out like a good Guidance counsellor.

"We've figured out Oma's thinking. Stick to the floodplains, blend with groups, hide in the woods. We don't need to walk every centimetre, do we?" Judy asked. "Tomorrow we could ride to Riesa with the bags."

I didn't answer right away. It felt like cheating since we were slated to walk every day, but then, another day with the raw blisters might have done me in. I stared at the Meissen Citadel across the way.

"What do you say? Are you going to be stoic or sensible?" Judy prompted.

I turned to Judy with a smile. "If the luggage driver will take us, we ride." Hey, I was flexible.

We rode to Riesa with blisters swathed and busted luggage. There the manager at the Hotel Mercure, the charming Frau Sylvia Brauening, briefed me about her plans for what would be our first interview with an audience. She also arranged to have the broken suitcase fixed, to Judy's immense relief.

I was a little daunted by the plans Frau Brauening outlined. The next evening we were to meet a WWII period witness and her husband, a local historian, and amazingly enough, an American Consul driving from Berlin. He would accompany American Army personnel who wanted to sit in on our interview of the period witness. The American group was with the American Army Defence Prisoner of War and Missing Personnel Office. They continued the search for the fates of downed WWII airmen right into the present.

"Yes," I told the astounded Judy up in our room, "the Americans are still looking for their war dead."

Judy who had been flipping through the hotel's brochure suddenly yelled, "Bicycles! The hotel has bicycles. We can ride tomorrow."

"Isn't that even more cheating?" I asked.

"Not if injured. We'll go on the route Constanze planned, only on bikes."

The next day the skies were blue, the sun was warm and pedaling was a great relief from stepping. We laughed that we didn't know what day of the week it was. We did remember we were to make it to Muehlberg where a new driver was to pick us up. We gambled that this Herr Wolfgang Barth would have a car big enough to take both of us and the bicycles.

With the help of our metal steeds, we whipped through pleasant, flat countryside that took us away from the Elbe. We passed sleeping villages with neat houses. Occasionally there were derelict buildings, but I could not imagine Oma had ever wandered this far away from the river. In one small hamlet we talked briefly to a young man as eager to give directions as we were to see signs of life. We were only a few metres further along when we heard a shout.

"Hey, aren't you supposed to be walking?" a man in a yard yelled in our direction.

We stopped the bikes with a shudder of brakes, astounded at the man's question.There had been press coverage about our journey in a few local newspapers. Had this man read something about us being in the area? We were two unfamiliar ladies speaking from bike to bike, in English. That had to be it. Yes, the stranger in the yard had read the news about the Canadian ladies walking along the Elbe.

"We've been found out," I said aghast to Judy, "and in the middle of nowhere."

"*Guten Tag! Blasen*!"

I stammered a little about my blisters, worked in friendly greetings and then we put our feet to the pedals and shoved off. The man didn't disappear from our quickly snatched rear views for a while. Judy broke the silence of our energetic progress.

"Kinda nice that someone took note of our journey," she said riding up beside me. It was.

Judy's attention was almost immediately diverted by a sign for a restaurant called Hamburger Hof. "Finally, hamburgers!" she shrieked and picked up the pace. I saw her form become smaller ahead of me as we moved towards the outskirts of Muehlberg.

Old medieval Muehlberg was picturesque. We found Hamburger Hof on its main cobbled square. We took the hotel's locks and cautiously chained the bicycles to one of the buildings nearby that conveniently had a metal rail. We surveyed a comprehensive menu once seated inside the busy restaurant. Judy flipped it forwards and backwards. No hamburgers!

"No, madam, no hamburgers," said the waitress to Judy. Judy was motivated to attempt German to make the hamburgers materialize.

"I guess I'm the only Hamburger," I said. Judy had heard that joke too many times. I used to tell my students that since I was born in Hamburg, I was a hamburger. One of my few references to my German heritage was a self-deprecating joke.

"Not funny," Judy said crestfallen.

We waited for hamburger substitutes while a steady stream of locals came and went to cast ballots for mayor. We had arrived on election day and the restaurant was a polling station. By now the English-speaking ladies, stupid enough to have asked for hamburgers in Hamburger Hof, were pegged as tourists. The innkeeper sat near us and after a quick conversation that he initiated, he left to return with a stack of books. Our host was an amateur historian. Most of the material he heaped before us was about the Muehlberg prisoner-of-war camp where over 3,000 Allied soldiers died. There had been so many dead that they had simply ploughed them under, just as in Dresden. We had a 20 minute crash course on the horrors of Stalag IV-B Muehlberg that continued to be a place of horror right up to 1948. We handed back the books when I checked my watch. Our driver was to pick us up by the small church near the square. It was time to meet Herr Barth.

"Oh my god, the bicycle locks won't open," I said as I struggled with mine.

"We've got to get them off," Judy said earnestly. "We can't abandon the hotel bicycles." We fiddled and fussed and as we did a lady leaned out a second storey window right above us. A few young men passed by with female friends. They stopped to take the "Sword in the Stone" test made famous by the King Arthur legend. They pulled and struggled with the chains. Could one of them be the hero to free the bicycles? No luck. The bicycles held fast to the iron railing.

I started to fiddle again. My father had this low German expression, *Immer worschteln lassen,* to tell my mother to leave me alone to figure out things on my own. "Let her fiddle," he'd say. My father's faith in fiddling paid off that day. All of a sudden, I lifted my chain up over the seat and released bicycle number one. The lady in the window laughed lustily.

"Do that again," said Judy, also laughing. I freed bicycle number two with a little more gerrymandering. More raucous hoots emanated from on high.

"I can't get the chains off the railing though," I said still fiddling with the chains as Judy held the bikes steady.

"Leave them," Judy said. "It's time to find Herr Barth."

We arrived at the liaison spot and told the driver, who we had only just met, about our struggle to free the bicycles. We also explained that the chains remained prisoners. After Herr Barth got over the surprise of our having bicycles and after he fit them nicely into his van, he too wanted to try the "Sword in the Stone" test. He longed to be champion of the chains. He selected an assortment of tools from a chest in his van and with the two of us in tow strode ahead to the challenge.

The chains were no match for the determined Herr Barth. But, in fairness to the locks, they did not give in right away. There was still quite a bit of amusement for the lady in the window who had come back for Act II. Some of the young men who had failed the test on their way to vote, now strode back, puffed up by the continuing obstinacy of the locks. Then finally, the locks yielded and Herr Barth led the parade back to the van holding the chains aloft.

"I like this man," said Judy.

We discussed our next day's itinerary as Herr Barth drove through pleasant villages back to Riesa for our evening interviews. We had left enough time to clean up and have a snack, but as the elevator door opened, we saw uniformed U.S. Army personnel hover around an elegantly clad, short-haired octogenarian. She held court in the foyer. Hotel manager, Frau Brauening, made introductions and led us to a private meeting room.

Our WWII period witness Helga and her husband, Horst Gaebler, sat beside one another on a couch. Horst had the air of a military man; he easily carried off being the custodian of Helga's purse. Helga, who had hardly stopped to breathe during the transition from foyer to meeting room, seamlessly kept up her narrative. Frau Gabriele Teumer, the Chair of the Oschatzer *Heimatsverein*, a local history group, beamed. She was proud to have assembled this interesting cast of characters. I said a few words in greeting, the military men interjected a few questions, but mainly Helga held forth with a continuous story. She was proud to tell us her tales.

She started with her background and the first thing she said held my attention. Helga was born October 20, 1923 on a farm near Reppen, a village of 300 people. My mother was born in the village of Blankenese on the Elbe River on September 30, 1923. Helga and my mother were the same age. They were both period witnesses. I had not thought of my mother like that and yet she was no different than the others. Well older. Leonore, Eva and Siegfried had been children in 1945; my mother and Helga were 22-years-old.

"I was a group leader in the local *Bund Deutscher Maedel*, the BDM," Helga said and stopped when she noticed the blank eyes in the room. "You know it as The League of German Girls. It was the girls' equivalent to the Hitler Youth."

Forget that Helga and my mother were alike, I thought at that reference to the BDM. My mother was banished to stand in the school hall by herself while BDM girls sang songs, recited pledges and did obeisance to Hitler. My mother wasn't "Aryan" enough to be in the same classroom with girls like Helga.

"I did work service on a silkworm farm, for parachutes you know, and war service in a Torgau munitions factory. No use denying it. We were all enthusiastic about the Nazi Party in the 30s. People were happy for work." Helga said this quickly and with force, as self-justification. Then she moved to the story of Dresden.

"What happened in June?" I asked. I wanted to move her past the firebombing and towards the time Oma had come through Dresden after the war was over. Oma and my mother had survived *Operation Gomorrah,* the week long fire-bombing of Hamburg in July 1943. What Oma saw passing through the Dresden area in mid-June 1945 differed little from the devastation of Hamburg she'd seen in the summer of 1943.

I considered that Oma was likely in trauma overload by June 1945. She was already weighed down by the bombing of Hamburg and death in Theresienstadt. Then, at the end of the war, when liberation came, she heard about rapes in Theresienstadt and saw its victims. Military historian, Sir Anthony Beevor[11], used his significant reputation to expose the orgy of rapes perpetrated by soldiers of the Red Army as they crossed towards Berlin. Among the hundreds of thousands of women raped were concentration camp survivors.

I shifted my thoughts away from the horrific things Oma must have witnessed, to where we sat in Riesa. Helga had looked upward towards the hotel's ceiling, thinking, and then recalibrated to June 1945. "Well the front moved closer, faster. In June, refugees flowed past our farm in great numbers. When the Russians reached the Elbe, everything that could move was put into service: cars, motorcycles, horses and wagons, bicycles,

---

[11] Antony Beevor, *Berlin: The Downfall,* was published in 2002 by Viking Penguin. A large amount of Beevor's substantiating data came from Russian archives and the Eastern Documentation Section of the German Federal Archives, Berlin.

children's wagons and carts of all descriptions. Everyone wanted to flee. They'd heard about the retribution and the rapes."

Helga explained how Resi, a friend of hers, was with them for protection. Helga and Resi had to set up in the attic when her father installed a young Cologne mother and her three children in their room. The young woman had been raped by three Russians while sheltering at a neighbouring farm.

"Couldn't the farmer protect her?" I asked.

"They were blood hounds," Helga said. "The Russians followed the tracks of any woman they'd seen, no matter what her age. They sniffed out when the neighbour went to the fields and got her then."

My father told the Russians that Resi and me had gone to Oschatz.

"When are those pretty ones coming back?" the Russian soldiers persisted in asking almost daily. In one close call when Helga went outside, she spent the night in the cornfield.The Russians were too close for her to move without discovery.

Helga finally stopped talking. Then before anyone mustered a question, she pumped her hands to ward us off. She appeared to go through an index of stories in her mind, worried that she wouldn't get to the best one.

"Just one more incident from the time before Resi and I fled the Reppen area for good," she said. She looked directly at me and continued, "And this happened right at the time when your Oma was passing." And with that, she began again.

"Fourteen British RAF airmen arrived on foot from the prisoner of war camp at Muehlberg," Helga stopped and looked at Judy and me. "The place you two passed. And, like your Oma, these RAF had struck out on their own. While I talked with the British officer in charge, he kept fumbling with something in his pocket. He finally pulled up his watch, which he had attached to a string and then lowered it back down his pant leg into his sock. He laughed as he said, 'This is what I had to do to protect my watch from "friendly" Allies. The Russians are crazy about watches, clocks and bicycles, not just beauties like you.'"

Helga completed the story with details about how she had dressed in a borrowed British uniform with Resi as her nurse. They traveled with the Brits to get out of the dangerous Russian occupied area. They had only made six kilometres towards Oschatz when two Italian men stopped them. These men had received refuge at Helga's farm the week before. They'd stolen a photo of Helga with her fiancé Horst, dressed as a German lieutenant. They said Horst was SS.

"We take you to Russians," they threatened.

During the argument three armed American soldiers showed up. They sent the Italians packing; they decided they were better protectors than the Brits.

"We have guns," the Americans pointed out to the British PoWs. Helga and Resi traveled with them for a few kilometres. Then a truck arrived and took the Americans away. Helga and Resi were left to fend for themselves during two more weeks of dangerous travels.

Helga's descriptions of the dangers posed by soldiers made Oma's predicament very real. More than one period witness had talked about the period of lawlessness that spring and summer of 1945 but Helga's stories hammered home the precariousness of the situation.

Before the hotel party broke up, an American officer named Sanchez asked questions about downed pilots, but Helga didn't have useful information for him. Then there were thanks all the way around before Helga took me aside to present me with a book she had written titled, *Geschichten/Stories.* The party dissolved with Horst still carrying Helga's purse. There was a powerful life force in Helga's wake as she walked away.

That night I read some of Helga's stories. Her father had been a guard at Stalag IV-G Oschatz and their farm had been given two slave labourers. Helga had gone from Group Leader of the local League of German Girls to war work in support of the regime. She was one of the "oldest" of the period witnesses. Like my mother she had been 22 at the end of the war.

It was hard to see Helga as an innocent, and yet, I appreciated the candour with which she shared her stories. She had not shirked from stating her involvement in the war or that of her father. My mother had said nothing about what she saw or experienced during WWII. I was left to puzzle out why Helga talked and my mother was silent. Perhaps, it was as simple as who processed and who did not process their experiences. My mother's trauma was unprocessed right up to her death and had found its outlet in tirades. The period witnesses were providing helpful comparative insights.

Chapter Thirteen: What a Difference a Day Makes

The saviour of the chains showed up early. Herr Barth pointed out the large Roland statue as we rolled into the main square of Belgern en route to our start. The "Roland" was a sandstone-coloured knight statue about five metres tall.

"They're all different," he said. "This Roland is the only one in Saxony."

"What do they mean?" I asked as I peered at the reddish man towering before us.

"A Roland statue meant the town had privileges in medieval times. For example, they could mint and issue coins," Herr Barth said like a good tour guide.

We got out of the car to take photos with the tall knightly figure erected in 1610. It was fun to pose in a small town that had "made it" in the 17th century. Herr Barth bade us good day and he was off. Judy and I trod Belgern's ancient cobbled streets. We passed ladies on the way to the main square. I tried not to stare, but I saw in their faces the same women who had gone to market for centuries. These were the faces I recognized from my German childhood. Faces like my mother's school friends Ingrid, Herta and Hilde and her Aunts Dora and Lina. I was among kith and kin.

We found the path along the river a few minutes later. We had 25 plus kilometres to go to make it to Torgau. Alas for my poor feet! We were not very far along the path when I pulled Judy's sleeve to say, *sotte voce*, "My god, Judy, it's a stork!"

"Where?" she asked.

"In the high grass, left of the path." I fumbled for my camera which I had strung around my neck. "Damn!" I cursed. The black and white wonder on spindly legs ambled out of range before I had my camera. I was disappointed because my mother always made a great to-do about storks. To see them was good fortune. I wanted to capture that good fortune. I wanted, even after my mother's death, to have the good fortune of her smile upon me. For reasons known only to her, I had never been what she wanted. She told me so in great angry outbursts. "I wish you'd never been born," she shouted at me when I'd disappointed her and didn't drive her to where she wanted. Smile upon me now, oh storks of Germany, I said silently to myself.

We went on at that point, stork-less. The path turned away from the river, but rounded back to where there was a tall, wide mound running along it that obscured the view of the water. I took to walking on top of this grassy mound, called a dyke, because the day was suddenly hot. There was a breeze from the Elbe that provided fresh air, flavoured with gnats. Judy, who a short while before had stepped into a bog going through a muddy construction site, had a soaker. She was trying to dry out. She kept to the lower paved path not wet with dew.

I described the Elbe vistas to her as we walked, high and low, in tandem. The river was wide and scenic as it curved through flat lands. It was a painterly subject with willow groves casting shadows over the water and fluffy clouds in a cerulean sky. We passed several communities that provided scenic sight lines in the distance. Finally, a restaurant sign appeared along the path and we searched for the eatery in a small hamlet. The place we sought was very ordinary. Judy used the time we waited for service to go through the travel descriptions for the day. I scoped out what appealed to the blue-collar workers concentrated on wolfing down their grub.

"We can cut off 1.5 kilometres by detouring through here," she pointed as she laid down the crumpled map before me. "We'd miss lakes—"

"You had me at cut off, " I cut in.

We were on the shoulder of a busy road when we started again. Soon the construction marked on Constanze's map forced us into farmers' fields.

"Still okay," I noted. The deeply furrowed fields were remarkably dry and we were safe from the crazy traffic. The large construction project on the other side of the road was dormant.

"I bet that's why there's no construction." Judy pointed at a fenced-in area around a fresh, deep excavation. Six persons peered at the walls sheared off by an earth-moving machine.

"Looks like a forensic team, all in white like that," I said.

"They're sifting something very carefully," Judy noted as we neared.

"Wonder if they found human remains?" I asked.

"Can't very well ask, can we?" Judy noted. "Hey, found any murdered persons from WWII?" With Oma's journey through the Sudeten Hills in mind, that was exactly what we thought.

Once back on the path that Constanze had set, we passed through a well-kept community with an austere, square church sitting conservatively on a sparsely adorned lot. Hmm, I thought, architecture devoid of ornamentation? This was Protestant country.

"Martin Luther, we're coming!" I shouted to Judy's amazement. She didn't know what was going on because we'd not discussed the Lutheran-Catholic geographic divide in Germany. I had Catholic relatives in the Cologne area but north of that, all my relatives were Lutheran, except for my Jewish Oma. Germany tended to be religiously divided north and south between Catholic and Protestant.

Judy, too, was excited because we finally saw Torgau in the distance. After a whole day of prancing on dykes, plodding through fields and passing orderly small hamlets, we saw the skyline of Torgau as a pinpoint on the horizon. We still needed to traverse vast suburban flat lands to advance on the metropolis, but, at least our goal was in sight.

I remembered a photo I saw on my laptop the night before when we reached a bench by the Elbe River in Torgau. We had made it to the abutment of the bridge where the Allies and Russians met in April 1945 to shake hands. There, on that bench, we rested under the shadow of towering Castle Hartenfels. I could feel the import of the place. I felt the relief in the soldiers and commanders when the Russians and their Allies closed the gap on the Germans. They could drive them to Berlin and final defeat.

It was time to find our hotel when the sun settled into late afternoon. We wended through the medieval streets of old Torgau. The hotel was one of the oldest buildings in town. Judy had battled a serious cold for a few days, and after our usual clean-up, wander-about and meal, we headed to bed. We arose to face yet another wet day of walking. Judy went on strike. Not right away. She was far too nice for that. She seized the opportunity to mutiny when we got lost trying to find the Elbe route that Constanze had outlined for us for that day.

"We'll do more good looking around Torgau than walking all day in the pouring rain," Judy said as we wandered aimlessly in search of the route. I knew she was right; we headed back.

We had seen part of a prison on our sodden, outward path that day just before the city park. Later, when we toured the exhibition *Traces of Injustice* in Castle Hartenfels, we saw a photo of the row of doors we had spotted that morning. They were part of Fort Zinna, the German military prison that took over Castle Hartenfels during WWII. Fifty thousand German soldiers were prosecuted in the castle for dereliction of duty; 20,000 *were executed.* The German commanders tolerated no infractions; showed no mercy. If a command was not followed, the soldier was usually found guilty and shot. As the war progressed, German soldiers questioned their commands, many of which seemed futile. Compared to only 300 Allied soldiers executed by their own troops during WWII, the figure of 20,000 Germans executed was staggering. It fit well with one of the few war stories my father told.

My father, the son of a First Engineer in the German merchant marine, had been unwilling to serve the Nazi cause. He objected for political reasons, but he also hoped to stay in Hamburg as a comfort to my *Mischling* mother who had lost her father to cancer in August 1939.[12] My mother and father met in

[12] My mother's father, Alfred Schilling, was Lutheran and a WWI veteran. When he died a week before the outbreak of WWII, the "protection" he had afforded his wife and daughter was fragile.

the same cemetery where my father's mother had been buried in the spring of 1939[13]. They took separate trains to meet in the woody groves of Ohlsdorf Cemetery.

Just after his 21st birthday in 1941, my father was brought into a police station with other "slackers". They marched the reluctant conscripts to the firing range in the precinct's basement; told them to face the wall. My father heard guns cock, then thunder. One man dropped. As the man moaned from the pain of pellets in his back, those who faced the wall heard the shout: "Do you want to serve your country?"

Well, they did.

My father reluctantly became a German soldier in February 1941, despite being secretly engaged to a *Mischling*/half-breed, an engagement specifically prohibited by the law for *The Protection of German Blood and German Honour.* The love my parents had was "criminal", so much so that at one point my "Aryan" father was disciplined for being seen in the company of a *Mischling*/mixed breed person. They did not marry officially until after the war.

Judy and I found all facets of Castle Hartenfels' history well-documented, but, the turbulent events of April 1945 dwarfed the stories of previous centuries. When Hitler's command went out, "Back into the Reich", German soldiers retreated from wherever they were to take a last stand for the Fatherland. The entire region around Torgau had been in uproar. German citizenry fled from the Russians and other Allied forces. Whom to fear more?

German army units fell back towards Berlin; other units drove concentration camp internees and forced labourers on death marches further into the Reich. The Germans evacuated the PoW camps in Muehlberg and Torgau; they left behind the dead and dying. In this madness of movement, Hitler and the Nazi leadership demanded that soldiers and citizens fight to the last person. They were prepared to shoot those who did not heed this command.

---

13 My paternal grandmother died as the result of a reaction to a penicillin injection. Her husband's ship had been quarantined due to an unknown illness. When she became seriously ill, doctors felt that penicillin might help her.

My father had a story from those desperate days near the end of the war. His took place in the Rhine River Valley. While his unit was in retreat from the *Battle of the Bulge,* he temporarily left it to go to his uncle's atelier in Vogelsang on the outskirts of Cologne. Death was all around him. He didn't know if he'd live to see another day. He thought it worth the risk to detour briefly to see the uncle who was like his father while the "First Engineer" was at sea.

My father found his uncle's studio empty. Disappointed, he sped towards the last intact bridge over the Rhine River. He was desperate to catch up with his unit. Corpses of soldiers were strung up on lampposts all along his path. Signs fluttered on their lifeless bodies. They said, "I am a traitor" and "I was not with my unit."

German soldiers feared their commanders during the period of chaotic retreat. Many stripped off their uniforms to blend with the refugees. My father barely made it back in time to cross the last bridge over the Rhine, one that the Germans had not dynamited to slow the Allies' pursuit.

On April 24, 1945, the retreating German army dynamited the bridge at Torgau leaving behind a swirl of anxiety among civilians and refugees. Non-combatants wanted to stay out of the combat zone but they did not know how to do that as it seemed to be all around them. Russian and American soldiers embraced in the ruined girders of that bridge on April 25, 1945. On April 14, 2008, Judy and I sat happily where history had been made. The day after that on April 15th we knew the secrets of Castle Hartenfels, a place of immense suffering. What a difference a day had made.

The rain break in Torgau afforded rare reflection time, but we had a timetable. We had to reach Wittenberg where my friend Ludwig Hendricks would join us. I had met Ludwig and Renate Hendricks when she was on a fact-finding mission to the Durham Board of Education. Durham had won the prestigious Carl Bertelsmann Prize in 1996 for Innovative School Systems. Renate was then chair of all the Parent Councils in Germany and she wanted to see what this particular Canadian Board of

Education was doing right. I was a vice-principal in the Durham Board at that time and showed Renate and Ludwig around Pine Ridge Secondary School, then dubbed "the school of the future". After her work with the Parent Councils Renate was subsequently twice elected Member of Parliament for Rhine-Westfalen.

We had kept in touch the whole time, 12 years by 2008. Ludwig and Renate were my representative post-war "modern Germans". They were cognizant of Germany's dark history, acknowledged the need to teach it, but, unlike me, had not taken it upon themselves to shoulder the guilt of a time period from before they were born. I wanted to be like them and yet I was not. But then, they didn't have the dual identity of being Jewish and German. Their parents had not undergone firebombing and concentration camps. Most significantly, they did not suffer from the hand-me-down trauma that was my baggage. I had more reconciliation work than they.

Duty to the government kept Renate in Bonn, but Ludwig would walk with us. He wanted to explore art on exhibit in Wittenberg; he was a connoisseur and a collector of many precious things from art to books and gold jewelry. Ludwig would travel to Wittenberg by train.

Herr Barth worked out where we had to start to be on time to dress for dinner with Ludwig. He edged us to a start point at Esnig where the bicycle path was close to the Elbe. We spent the next three hours on broad Elbe flood plains. The willows, sheep, farmyards, and mistletoe-laden trees blended together, especially since we always seemed to see them in relentless, leaden-cloud and spitting-rain conditions. I didn't feel guilty trying to speed past these repetitive sights, as Oma had also found rides and shortcuts. At this point of the walk, I felt that I did not need to inventory every rough-barked willow under which she might have sat. I savoured the experience holistically.

Eventually we saw the tiny spires of Wittenberg beyond several bends in the river. Our host at the Black Bear Hotel, Herr Gerhardt Koppe, moved us away from the construction at the front of the hotel. The town was putting in an open watercourse to reflect, in an upscale fashion, the medieval city when people threw swill into an open gutter. Judy and I had barely completed our beautification before the appointed time to meet Ludwig.

Ludwig was in the restaurant when we got there. We unleashed *Gemuetlichkeit* with a few drinks and then toured the anti-fascist art exhibition Ludwig came to see. The works in the City Hall Gallery did not disappoint. We loved the Lea Grundig pieces from her etching cycle, *Under the Swastika*. Grundig was a talented, persecuted artist, a "degenerate" according to the Nazis, the same way my father's Uncle Willy Fick in Cologne had been.

Grundig was tagged "degenerate" as a Jew; my Catholic great-uncle was "degenerate" for his politically charged dada art activities. Dada had been an anti-art (and anti-war) movement that exploded out of Zurich in 1916. It swept up artists in Cologne between 1916 and the death of my great-aunt Angelika Hoerle in 1923. Angelika, after whom I was named, was Willy Fick's artist sister and had been called by the local newspapers, "the German mistress of dada." I was preparing an exhibition for her for 2009 and had already started the research before the walk.

From the City Hall gallery, a quick jaunt through the pedestrian mall took us to Wittenberg's most famous tourist site. The big draw in Wittenberg were the doors to the church where Martin Luther posted the 95 theses which started the Protestant Reformation. Metal doors stood in for the wooden ones upon which Luther had nailed his *Diet of Worms*. We discussed our disappointment in the modern substitute doors and then hurried back to the Potato Restaurant where we were registered for supper. The newly formed group gelled further as we enjoyed a supper flavoured by artsy conversation. Ludwig would join us the next day to walk after I was interviewed by a reporter from a radio station that served the Dessau/Wittenberg/Kloeden area.

It turned out that the ebullient radio personality, Frau Grit Lichtblau, and our Black Bear host, Herr Koppe, knew one another. They were in an animated conversation when Judy and I arrived from the breakfast room. After a comfortable, flowing interview, we shared more stories with Herr Koppe who enthusiastically volunteered to tour us through the area and drive to our starting point near Griebo.

The first stop on Herr Koppe's tour was the small suburb of Wittenberg called Apollensdorf where he lived in what was once his mother's house located directly on the shores of the Elbe. He said that at about the same time the Russians and Americans met at Torgau, they also met in his mother's basement. He claimed Allied and Russian soldiers rowed across the Elbe and a few made it across on horseback.

I took his story as local puffery, to outdo Torgau, but later research on my notepad showed an American soldier with the 83rd Infantry division, the Thunderbolts, had recorded on the back of a map that he met up with Russian soldiers at Apollensdorf, 13:30, April 30th, 1945. His son found the map many years after the war. It appeared history was made in many different places along the Elbe at roughly the same time, even in Herr Koppe's basement.

Imposing black metal gates, remnants of a forced labour camp, stood not more than a few metres from Gerhardt Koppe's house. His mother had told him that frail, downcast labourers went by the house daily, to and from work. A later look-up showed that there was a sub-camp of Flossenberg Concentration Camp on the outskirts of Wittenberg. Slave labourers worked there for Arado *Flugzeugwerke GmbH* producing planes for the Luftwaffe. Not long after WWII, the site of the camp was covered over with slag from neighbouring chemical plants. But for Herr Koppe, we would never have known the significance of the grassy knoll at Apollensdorf.

Herr Koppe drove us next to a narrow, wooded path at the end of which lay the Elbe. We headed off to walk 12 kilometres back to Wittenberg. We passed more industry than usual and all too frequently the path diverted us back to the major thoroughfare that had taken us out of Wittenberg. Ludwig appeared to flag, but he did not let on. No way! He was committed.

The decision to tour the former East German Republic's DDR Museum in Wittenberg was a good one. We journeyed down into memory as we descended from the fourth floor. The rooms were stuffed with kitsch and period pieces. I loved the tile stoves, *Kacheloffen.* I used to melt and mould patches of candle wax on the warm tiles in the corner stove in the living room of our apartment on Papendamm in Hamburg. It was a pleasant memory.

The museum displayed a doll's carriage exactly like the one I had received for Christmas when I was three. My parents had not understood why I howled. I was pacified only after they tucked the carriage in bed with me. It was one of the times I had proven "difficult". I wrote about a more serious incident when I later ran away from daycare:

> *I had pulled a suitcase full of wrath upon myself by absconding from a mandated nap session. I was not good with rules. I had wandered away from the lumps under blankets on the floor when the lights went off. Lockdowns for daycare did not exist in 1950s Hamburg, Germany.*
>
> *I bowed slightly to pass under the turnstile to gain entry to the subterranean and surface transit trains that crisscrossed the bomb-damaged city. I spent a few hours riding into the countryside to catch sight of the bushes and berries that enchanted my parents in our garden plot. I shifted seats frequently. When one family got up to leave, I found another. I reasoned in my five-year-old way that this would keep me safe. I have no recollection of how I was found or returned.*
>
> *The next day I swung my legs back and forth as I sat on the wooden bench outside the headmistress's office. I awaited a repeat of the rant from the night before. I was picturing my red-cheeked mother and her jabbing, pointy finger, when I was called into the private enclave of brown-paneled power. I knew I had to apologize.The headmistress forgave me. My mother never did. She had worked herself into frenzy worried at the thought that one of Hamburg's homeless men had snatched me into the ruins to replace a "lost" child. She was relieved when I was found, but after that she kept hissing out of her pinched lips, "How could you!"*

The many kitchen setups in the DDR Museum stirred more memories. They were full of items from the kitchen of my childhood: a meat grinder, all sizes of metal funnels, aluminum potato mashers and pots and a wood-burning stove. The past flashed before me through kitchen accoutrements. I heard Oma vent her frustrations as she pounded meat down into the grinder, the meat she'd prepared according to grandfather Jakob Skrainka's kosher recipe. She used bay leaves, paprika and all spice. My history linked back to Holesov with spicy sausages.

More perambulations in old town Wittenberg took us down *Judengasse*/Jew Street. There the good citizens of Wittenberg retained, among the cobblestones, the medieval image entitled *Judensau*/Jewish sow. It was a reminder of the past's well-ripened anti-Semitism, including Martin Luther's, and a warning to the present. We continued our walk around town but now I was ready to collapse. Ludwig kept going. He was made of the right stuff after all. He had three pieces of scrumptious pastry at the coffee break. Then with a quick embrace, he, like the past, was gone.

But, the past was not gone, not really. People I met, period witnesses, art, artefacts, ruins, sights along the river, they were conduits to memories. I realized that Germany was not just the first seven years of my life. Oma's and my parents' lives in Germany were the foundations of my own. Germany was a part of me.

Chapter Fourteen: Where's the Ferry?

We got back from the Black Bear's breakfast room to see the phone light blinking.

"Robbie, I bet. He's not missed a hotel yet," I said. Robbie had followed Constanze's trip plan since we left Prague. He called us in each new overnight location. I dialed him back.

"Yes, Robbie, your gals are safe. No, nothing new about Oma in Wittenberg and the Elbe's been the same flat terrain for ages." Pause. "Yes, we're having fun. But know what? There's always a local who wants to tell us about a forced labour, PoW, or concentration camp nearby—a satellite of something or other. We can't go 25 kilometres without a reminder—" I'm cut off. "Yes, yes, I know you told us..." And thus it went.

I stopped my morning preparations to consider the pervasiveness of WWII stories that arose from the Elbe landscape. Was it strange? WWII surrounded us in Ontario. There was Defence Industries Ltd., a munitions factory in Ajax, Camp X a spy camp in Whitby, No 20 Elementary Flying Training School (EFTS) in Oshawa and Camp 30, a PoW camp in Bowmanville, all within 25 kilometres of where I grew up and where we had both taught. Judy had a comeback to this WWII inventory.

"The difference," said Judy, "is that people in Canada don't know. I doubt anyone at our school could tell you about two of those things you mentioned. The war wasn't fought on Canadian soil; it didn't resonate in the same way."

"I've certainly never pointed out anything related to WWII to anyone," I said.

"Yet here in Germany," Judy continued, "every day we get a tip. Mind you, most people know we're searching for the past, but, still, the WWII past is more present here. Everyone wants to let you know about every Nazi camp, factory or even hut. We'd walk right by them if it weren't for people pointing them out."

"Yes," I said, "it's weird because you'd think they'd want to hide them."

The pleasant Herr Barth arrived at the hotel at that point in our discussion and we needed to get to our start point. Judy was determined to find the small lane, our furthest point forward from the day before. We started on a path considerably above the Elbe, and although it would probably not have been Oma's path, it was pleasant. We were shielded from industrial lands by significant woods.

It was another of those misty, wet mornings that traveled with us. Fairly soon I spotted a flat-bottomed Czech barge on the hard-working Elbe far below us and although this was not rare, it looked very scenic framed by the verdure of the budding spring forest.

We passed small settlements of picturesque single-storied houses seeming as ancient as the hills around them. The kilometres trundled along. Then the ochre Anhalt Castle raised its bulk above the rest of the landscape. We passed it by. No sightseeing for us. We did slow down to read interpretive panels at an allee adorned with gnarled, severely pruned, ancient head willows.[14] I translated the text.

"The willows get pruned once a year, the way people cut their mulberry trees back to a nub in Canada. They use the prunings for basket weaving and chair caning."

"What do these pictures show?" Judy asked. She was a few panels ahead.

"The willow switches can be woven into fish-and-eel traps. They also form buildings. See here. There are reed-like forms in the wall construction in this photo."

"I guess this panel means shallow-bottomed boats," Judy said and pointed.

---

[14] Osier willow, *salix wiminalis*, are often pollarded before they start to grow again.

"They're called coracles. They're useful in shallow waters and estuaries of rivers."

Judy turned from the panels and said with a snort, "And here you told me that the main role of all those water-sucking willows was to act as inspiration for romantic landscape painters. Didn't you say that Caspar David Friedrich was one?"

"Good memory, Jude," I replied.

Judy wandered towards the ferry landing area as I continued to read. I failed to notice the ferry's approach from the far side of the swiftly moving river. Judy called and I rushed towards her. I stepped onto a metal platform assuming that we waited on the dock to be let on the ferry. I looked around for the ferry entrance and all I saw was a small hut-like room. Aha, I thought, I found the seats for the crossing. I went in. I looked at the personal paraphernalia all around me in the small sitting area. I was confused.

"Where's the ferry?" I shouted to Judy, as I hurriedly exited.

"It's all the ferry," said Judy. She smiled broadly, stomped on the black metal and pointed to its edge. The ferryman, whose roost I had invaded, looked at me quizzically.

"I thought we were on the dock on this black thing," I said sheepishly.

From that point on all Judy had to say was, "Where's the ferry?" and we dissolved into laughter.

We saw this type of pulley ferry, called a *Gier* ferry, or flying bridge, several times again. The pullies took advantage of the river's currents to save time. The current at that spot near Anhalt was so swift that the ferry had previously taken 40 minutes to cross. With the use of heavy cables and an anchored pulley system, the ferry delivered customers to the other side in five minutes, for 50 German pennies.

We pursued a ramrod-straight path through a heavily logged forest once on the other side. I focused on the bright yellow, white, and cerise flowers that carpeted the earth where trees had been culled. The Elbe was nowhere in sight as we made our way towards the UNESCO-designated World Heritage Site called the Gardens of Woerlitz and Dessau. A large scenic vista opened suddenly after we had been closed in by trees for a while. In the sweep of that clearing we noticed dark threatening clouds and a sign for the gardens. We had arrived.

"This isn't what I expected of a garden," noted Judy as she looked at the open areas broken here and there by large trees.

"I guess we're used to the small, rail-corridor gardens," I said. "They're more colourful."

"At the very least, I expected flowerbeds." Judy looked around, disappointed.

"Well, from what I read last night, Duke Franz from Anhalt started these gardens back in the 1700s and he had other things in mind." I explained, "He visited English gardens. Loved the Italian architecture in Rome. He decided to plant rare trees, planned pathways wide enough for a carriage and then 'posed' sculptures and Italianate structures to create panoramas for his rides out into his curated countryside."

We passed through strategically placed, fairy-tale structures, suitable backdrops for princes and princesses, Duke Franz creations.

"Watch out for Rumpelstiltskin," I warned. "He's sure to appear in the next clearing." And with that, I started to sing. The German walking song evoked memories of marches through parkland with my brother and parents. My father had only Sunday as a full day off from his job. We would go into the countryside to walk and sing as much as the weather allowed. I could still sing most of those marching songs, and I loved to walk. There were good memories from my German past.

Judy and I walked right past our day's destination caught up in song and laughter. We had to double back to the brick wall that kept Woerlitz from prying eyes. When we entered the town across what must have been a moat in days of yore, we ran smack dab into—

"A pastry shop!" Judy shouted and ran over to the window displaying tortes, strudels, sponge cakes and chocolate confections.

"Journeys end in—" I was about to quote, but Judy cut me off again.

"Pastry tasting?"

We headed into the sweet-smelling café for a treat we had earned with a walk. We found the Park Hotel after a sampler of rich tortes and a taste of strong, aromatic coffee. Astonishingly, we were the hotel's only guests. Our footsteps echoed in the long empty corridors.

"The town looked quiet," I said as we stared over the balustrade of our balcony, "but..." I let my word hang in the air.

"Well?" Judy said as she looked out with me.

"I'm upgrading its status to deserted."

Back in the room I picked up tourist brochures laid out for what the hotel's management hoped would be a busier season ahead. "Now here's something." I held out a brochure. "There's an exhibition of Jewish life in the Anhalt era. According to the pamphlet, the display is open in the synagogue, right now while we're here."

The girl at the desk indicated that the synagogue mentioned in the brochure was nearby, down *Graben*/Moat Street. We followed her directions, and circled a cream-coloured round building. We circled it again. There was no discernible entry point. I expressed my disappointment to the hotel's young desk clerk who politely directed me to the town's information centre.

At the tourist information desk, I made a show of having traveled all the way from Canada to be disappointed to find the synagogue closed. The lady in charge had no explanation as to why the exhibition was not open. She bustled off into a back room to find literature about the synagogue and the history of the Jews in the area.

"The last Jewish person in Woerlitz died in 1910, madam," she said in stilted English. She emitted a strained smile. She was relieved that the citizens of Woerlitz did not have to bear guilt for the misdeeds of the Nazis. The Jews were already gone.

"As a matter of fact," the lady added, "on *Kristallnacht* in 1938, a park official saved the synagogue. He held the synagogue's doors shut from the inside to prevent vandals with torches from gaining access." Now her smile was genuine. She had found a local hero.

In the literature the lady provided, I read later that despite the park ranger's heroics, the synagogue was later stripped down, its wooden structure used for building materials elsewhere. We had circled a re-build. Of the many Jewish gravestones in Woerlitz, some that dated back to medieval times, only 310 fragments remained. The rest were used to pave the courtyards of the good citizens of Woerlitz. Quite the track record, Woerlitzers!

Over supper, Judy and I discussed that nothing in Woerlitz indicated that Jewish citizens ever lived there, including the synagogue which had no signage and was closed. The two or three pre-season tourists we heard, gabbed contentedly behind a screen of rhododendrons. They were within a stone's throw of the synagogue yet did not know it. The Jews were gone.

The next day was a simple 20-kilometres day through more UNESCO gardens. The beginning route towards Vockerode abutted farmers' fields separated by copses of bushes. Small birds flitted in and out of the shrubbery. We saw what appeared to be large cone-shaped beehives in the distance. The structures were much smaller as we got closer.

"Single-seat crematoria," I said sarcastically.

"That's a terrible thing to say."

"Well, it's Hitler's birthday today," I replied. "Negative vibes, I guess."

And with that, Judy was off racing up a hill to see a small sparkling lake held back by a dyke. I continued on the official path into the first of the deep and dark forests that marked our day. It was not long before we were surrounded by the venerable trees that probably felt the hand of the duke 300 years before. There was something magical about the strange convoluted forms of the ancient trunks. These were trees for fantasies. I saw hidden, twisted faces trapped inside them. *Grimm's Fairy Tales* had deep roots within me.

"Come out, come out, whoever you are," I called to the tree spirits in a sing-song voice. At that exact moment some heavy branches rubbed together with a ghastly groaning.

"What's that?" Judy asked startled.

"You never know."

"These certainly aren't the forests of Ontario," Judy said looking up at the looming trees with lots of space underneath them.

"No, these woods are orderly, and occupied," I said. I looked around. Foresters had culled brush and harvested elderly stock. The neat piles of logs and brush spoke of control. "This is a forest for lurkers. Shh!" I gestured with a finger to my lips. "The foresters are watching." I bent conspiratorially towards her. "They're hiding behind the massive, dark, gnarled trunks all around us."

Judy was glad to get out of the thickest part of the woods.

Soon we saw signs of rivers glinting through the trees, surprisingly, both on the right and left. I looked at Constanze's map. The Mulde and Elbe Rivers were in the area, but I couldn't make out which flowed where. We assumed the river to our left was the Elbe, as we occasionally spotted a barge on it. The Elbe was a working river.

We were never far from the creative touches of Duke Franz von Anhalt as we marched along. We passed sculptures and buildings the Duke erected to add to his pleasure of experiencing the cultivated wilds. Our stomping feet rarely paused. We commented on herons, buildings, strange trees and weather conditions as we made our way towards Dessau. I remarked that I saw an exit turnstile ahead.

"That," said Judy scornfully, "is a pile of logs."

I saw she was right when we got closer.

"Is that a mirage too?" I asked. I pointed further on where I had spotted a snack hut sprouting from the forest floor.

"That's real," Judy said. She bounded ahead in anticipation of food and facilities.

"Now don't go asking for hamburgers," I teased.

"And you," she said back over her shoulder, "don't ask for the ferry."

After a coffee and *Bratwurst*, we were off for more kilometres of dark, groomed forests and soggy plains until we finally crossed a wooden bridge.

"That bridge is our cue for Dessau," I said as I scanned Constanze's directions. The path took us through an extensive garden village containing a frenzy of flowers. We knew we were in Dessau proper when we passed the city slaughterhouse built in 1899, the year Oma was born. Amazingly in that era, a slaughterhouse merited ornate, red-brick construction. Slaughter was deceptively contained by beautiful brickwork.

Getting to the hotel was not easy. We wearily recalculated several times, the way a GPS does. Once we finally arrived, Judy headed to the sauna and I to my laptop. In between, Wolfgang Barth called to arrange pickups for our next two days. And of course, our intrepid supporter, Robbie Lavack called.

"It's Hitler's birthday today and we're in the city whose city council voted 20-5 to demolish the Bauhaus buildings back in 1932," I told Robbie. Talk, talk, talk on the other end, and then I added, "It's ironic, because the Bauhaus is a huge part of their tourist revenue today."

The next day we walked in rare sunshine. A broad bridge took us over extensive rail yards and past the Georgium Castle to the main Bauhaus buildings. Judy went into the display with English signage and I went on the guided tour in German. We compared notes in the Cellar Café, naturally over strudel.

"My displays were about the teachers and students and what they learned and accomplished with unique materials and utilitarian design," Judy said.

"I saw Walter Gropius' office, the teaching building, the residence and the student mess which held only 100 people and had to have many sittings to get through meals for 600 students. During the Bauhaus heyday, students attended three-month sessions."

"We saw interesting lighting and furniture experiments," Judy added.

I led Judy outside to the square in front of the Bauhaus complex to show what I'd found interesting when the tour leader pointed it out.

"The bases of the main buildings are recessed to make the white buildings above seem to float in the morning fogs wafting in from the Elbe and the Mulde. We saw that fog just this morning. It hung all around us!"

From Bauhaus ingenuity, we headed to the Masters' Houses, homes and studios for the artists who came to Dessau from Weimar in 1925. The city fathers had offered them a place to innovate, and homes. They took up the offer. The industrial town had raw materials with which they wished to experiment. As it turned out, Dessau was a poor choice for the predominantly Jewish group that included Paul Klee, Wassily Kandinsky, Leon Feininger, Oskar Schlemmer and Walter Gropius. The city council voted overwhelmingly to close the Bauhaus and dismiss its staff a mere seven years later. The Nazi Party instigated the motion. A great source of creativity and potential was no more.

We inspected the Masters' Houses and then checked our Dessau city map to find the best way to get to other Jewish sites. We found the Cantor's House easily, near the River Mulde. It stood by itself, an abandoned island in a city to which it bore no connection. Like the synagogue in Woerlitz, we circled it several times. It was closed.

By this time we were tired of the stop-and-go pace of city walking which differed from our marching rhythms, but we went on, determined to find one of the oldest Jewish cemeteries in the state. We followed the swiftly moving Mulde River which at that point had pretty garden allotments on its far side. We ignored the busy traffic flow to our right, a wilful compartmentalization. I understood that concept. My mother had compartmentalized. She was a model citizen in Whitby taking up valuable environmental causes and joined the Victoria Women's Association when I was at university and became president of the VWA for a few years. She was a wonderful person, in public. At home she provided unpredictable outbursts, sustained tirades, slamming of doors and tears. Judy broke into my thoughts about how easy it was to separate parts of one's life.

"There it is," Judy shouted and pointed. "Behind that high brick wall." Sure enough, she'd found what appeared to be a cemetery. We crossed the busy street and advanced along the wall that stretched for more than a city block. Finally, through a chink, I spied a pile of thin, grey headstones with Hebrew writing. They leaned and tumbled together as if for support. At this point, a nosy matron who had trailed behind us, came nearer. She approached after a few minutes and asked in formal German.

"Surely you do not wish to see the Jewish cemetery?" She asked that rhetorically with a hint of sneer. She did not understand interest in a Jewish cemetery. That was the past and most of the Jews of Dessau were gone. She babbled behind us as we three wandered along the wall. We arrived at the front gates of the cemetery when we turned the corner of the wall into a quieter side street. The gates were locked. There was no answer when we rang at a gatehouse. Judy tried another gate. Nothing. At that moment a police car went by at a slow pace that became slower as the two officers looked us up and down.

"Do you think someone called us in?" Judy asked quietly.

"I can feel an interrogation coming on. Get out your passport." I said this only half jokingly.

The police car moved down the street at a snail's pace.

"I think we're clear," Judy said as the car finally rounded the corner.

I looked behind us and the black-clad lady had disappeared. "At least, the police drove off the nosy lady," I said.

Judy tried a third, smaller gate in the wall. It opened into the well-kept cemetery. The bushes and grasses were neatly trimmed, the reddish sand paths were raked and a ladder leaned against a tree. We entered the quiet haven.

"A stairway to heaven," Judy commented as she made a beeline past the ladder to the very back of the cemetery. The wall there consisted of cemented-together fragments of broken gravestones. I stared at the ladder that had magically caught the sunlight. We had entered a holy place where it seemed possible to climb heavenward.

I read in the guidebook that the wall fragments came from gravestones toppled on *Kristallnacht*—a night in November 1938 when stone was broken and not just glass. The guidebook also said the Russians ploughed under the shattered grave markers from that night; the shards were later retrieved to make the wall.

"Judging by the very large number of stone splinters," I said as I looked at the long patchwork wall, "It took lots of people and a great deal of hate to do this amount of damage."

I consulted our guidebook further. Judy moved to a memorial sculpture, which, like the wall, was made up of shards of gravestones. "It's in a Star of David shape," Judy marveled as she walked around it.

"Looks like a bunker," I said. It was a shoulder-height structure of brick and gravestone pieces. The structure bore echoes of the concrete bunkers we'd seen when the Elbe was called the Labe in the Czech Republic. I had marveled at the bunker-like new synagogue in Dresden and the stark Richard Serra memorial called *Gravity* that David and I had seen at the Holocaust Museum in Washington, D.C. The bunker-star of Dessau fit with this Jewish art and architecture; it was "dark".

"The wall, the monument and the neat grounds," Judy said, breaking into my thoughts, "someone cares about these dead."

"And yet, the broken gravestones and the memorial are inside and do not face the city. What happened in 1938 is invisible to the good folk of Dessau, thanks to the wall."

"The Jewish past locked away," Judy mused.

"Unworthy of interest," I added.

"I guess our nosy lady said it all, didn't she?"

Next day, Herr Barth took us to a ferry that would transport us to the side of the Elbe on which Constanze had plotted a path to Barby. Breitenhagen's *Gier*, or pulley ferry, had only recently resumed operations after problems with the Elbe's higher than usual water level. I decided I would not intrude into the ferryman's private enclave on this crossing.

The passage was rapid and the ferry left us at the entrance to one of the oldest oak forests in Germany. A long, ochre-coloured path, made of interlocking paving stones, stretched before us.

"We're on the yellow brick road," I noted, "hopefully with all the adventure that means."

Judy saw only the massive forest with its tall, engulfing trees. "All alone with more of that damned creaking!" Judy said loudly as if to scare the spirits of the trees into behaving. We entered yet another sylvan world.

"You think we're alone," I said as I looked down at sparse growth and up at erect trees that blocked out the sky. But are we? Each tree here has a very distinctive mark. See," I said and pointed. "It takes substantial effort to carve all those blazes." We were surrounded by fervid tree husbandry and despite seeing no one, there was never a sense that we were alone in this frenetically worked forest.

The shaded path eventually spit us out to manicured villages that gleamed in sunshine. I noted that in one small stretch of houses, the rose and spirea bushes on the village median had been pruned with fascist zeal. The street was deserted.

"Where are all the gardeners doing this work?" I pointed to the scalped bushes just barely hanging onto a hint of greenery.

"There's no one here," Judy said as she looked around at the houses where no child played in neatly maintained gardens.

Then behind a set of the large doors that led to an enclosed courtyard we heard movements as unearthly as the wind rubbing tree limbs together. We rushed away from "the village of the dead" towards our next ferry. En route, I spotted it.

"Look, there. Finally, a stork!" I shouted and pointed. The creature was close by perched on the chimney of a single-storey building.

"That stork is close," Judy said. "See if he'll pose."

"Got it!" I shouted as I checked multiple shots. "My first digital stork!"

We had seen many camera-shy storks but this was the first to pose. A sign near the ferry told us that three of the four stork eggs in the area netted storks that year. We were barely across the river when we saw a stork's nest high on a pole, with another stork *in situ*.

"We've reached a stork-friendly land," Judy said as we approached the nest. "That has to be good luck. That's what you said, right?"

"That's what my mother told me." I smiled up at the stork family and felt the good fortune beam upon us. For a second, I felt my mother's presence and remembered a rare time of laughter with her. In 1988 we had travelled to Taipei, Taiwan to see the exhibition *The World According to Dada* because our family had loaned works to it. I'd seen my mother laughing on that trip! Just for the adventure, we'd taken a long boat ride to the Pescadores Islands between Taiwan and mainland China. The Pescadores were not equipped for English- or German-speaking tourists. For three days we pointed and did charades to get by for food and transportation. My mother had laughed with glee to discover that NO ONE understood us. The fun times with my mother were few, but I realized I should remember them—cherish them. Stopped on the path to admire the stork, I counselled myself: Let go of the hurt.

It was flat terrain along the flood plains at that point and Barby was soon visible. We entered through a gated opening in its thick medieval walls. The night before I had read that Barby had burned down in the late 1700s and was built up again over time by commercial shipping concerns that plied the Elbe. The manor house, originally built by the Dukes of Sachsen-Weissenfels, had gone through many permutations: from a religious institution, educational academy, and lazaretto[15], to a hostel for refugees. It was currently under construction again.

"They need even more construction than this," commented Judy as we passed the villa-like palace covered with scaffolding. Many other buildings in Barby were in poor repair.

"This whole town could benefit from an infusion of cash. It's picturesque-manqué," I noted.

"Let's blame the *Deut-sche Demo-kratische Re-publik* for that." Judy sounded out the German words as if she had marbles in her mouth. "Everyone blames the East Germans for poor infrastructure. You told me that during one of your history lessons," Judy said and rolled her eyes.

---

[15] A lazaretto is a hospital for those with contagious diseases; a building set apart for quarantine purposes.

Guilty, I thought. I did constantly bombard and weigh her down with information. Partly I did so as I couldn't keep from researching more about the past. Each day brought new discoveries that excited me. I had done the East and West Germany lessons for my own good as well as hers. I had spent the first years of my life in Hamburg in north Germany from 1946 to 1954. I had played in the heaped up rubble of bombed-out buildings that had not meant war to me because as a child I did not understand war. I visited Cologne, Coblenz, Munich and Luebbeck as a young woman in 1966. They were beautiful cities. I subsequently added Bonn, Dusseldorf, Aachen and Speyer with Ludwig and Renate Hendricks who went out of their way to show me the beauties of the back roads of Germany as well as tourist sites.

I had never visited East Germany and knew nothing about the Russian impact on it. I saw it now. We had walked for two weeks almost exclusively in the former East Germany. The Elbe River had formed a large part of the inner German border between East and West Germany for 40 years. The demarcation line was based on a British proposal for temporary post-war occupation zones but the East-West split became permanent when the British, French and American zones merged in May 1949 to create the Federal Republic of Germany. The Soviets created a communist dictatorship in response. An international border became a fact and life behind it in East Germany was organized along Stalinist lines. I saw how the construction from that era was cheaply done and the infrastructure neglected.

Our driver, Herr Barth, added personal details about the bleak economic legacy of the Russians. There was no work for young people. His two children left home to make their careers in West Germany. Herr Barth had two jobs to make ends meet. He had his driving business and he and his wife ran a small hotel at Strehla. Economic survival in the former DDR was a struggle.

We rose the next morning in Barby to a stream of light channeled in from our narrow window. Our bed and breakfast place backed onto the three-metres-thick town wall and the Elbe glistened in morning greeting through a barrel-vaulted casement going through brick and stone.

We were sad as we got ready. We would see the delightful Herr Barth for the last time that day. He would meet us via the same ferry we had used the day before and then he would drop us off and leave us to a new driver. That was how Constanze arranged it.

We sat talking nostalgically in the bed and breakfast's sunny courtyard when he arrived. We stalled a little to share more time with this warm, helpful man.

"You know the ferry man was still talking about you today," offered Herr Barth.

"Really? What's there to say?" asked Judy.

"Well, you astounded him. He kept repeating, 'Two ladies in black pants came across on foot. On foot,' he added again for emphasis. I told the ferry man, 'Those black pants are *my* ladies.'" He laughed heartily.

Wolfgang Barth had enjoyed the stalwart Canadian ladies he had shepherded from Riesa to Barby. He was sad to see the last of our adventure. We set off with heavy hearts. Herr Barth would leave us at the dam at Pretzien that was built to secure the lands around Magdeburg from Elbe flooding.

Judy and I hugged Herr Barth good-bye. It was uncharacteristic to hug someone with whom you were not on a "Du", or an informal, basis. My mother's northern German formality dictated distance and reserve. We could not help it though. We really liked this man who had guided us for over a week.

Herr Barth hugged us back.

The contact with drivers, even those we saw for short distances, provided an extra lens through which to process our walk experience. Judy and I discussed what we saw as we traveled along; we had my pre-trip and nightly research to annotate Constanze's daily trip section; period witnesses prompted deep dives into the past and then there were the memories that drew forth from my German roots. The friendly and chatty drivers, like Herr Barth, were "value added" They personalized contemporary life and they did it well.

Chapter Fifteen: Is the Trip Over?

Judy and I started towards Schoenebeck. The sun was out as we walked on a high, straight dyke that stretched into the distance. The strong wind soon moved us down to the dyke's sheltered lee. Eagles coasted in the thermals high above us. I favoured my right foot because of the continuing blisters but the sunshine took away the pain. We saw what we had been told were hunters' platforms not far along. These strange wooden lookout towers had proliferated since the forests on the approach to Woerlitz.

"Good thing it's not hunting season because we'd be dead ducks, even with our bright red and turquoise jackets," Judy said.

"Caught in the crossfire for sure," I said as two towers were within the scope of our vision.

Judy gestured to the nearest tower and I felt I should duck and keep my head down.

We deviated from the path in search of coffee at the village of Ranies. We approached an elderly farm couple who had opened their heavy, wooden, courtyard doors for a small, mechanized, farming vehicle to get out.

"Excuse me, sir. Where might we find a café?" I asked in polite, formal German.

The quasi-toothless man was struck dumb to be asked a question by a stranger. Judy and I walked on. I looked back, and yes, he had turned to stone. Well, it looked like it. He'd not moved from where he stood.

"They'll not soon open their doors again," quipped Judy.

"But, they'll talk about the black-pants ladies for years to come," I joked. "The ones who spoke to strangers."

The road led us out of Ranies, without coffee, to a path become an astrological chart that schematized the distance between planets. We found notations for Uranus and Pluto and then trudged wearily into the furthest reaches of the galaxy. We could not see a single spire or sign of Schoenebeck even at the borders of the known galaxy. I did notice something else.

"There are numbers on the trees. Look, they're all numbered with plaques," I said with disgust.

"We've seen that before," Judy said. "Why does it bother you?"

"Trees shouldn't be branded." I was huffy because she should have understood.

"They're probably valuable," Judy said scanning a tall, numbered tree.

"Still. There's something wrong when trees on remote, back routes in Germany, even valuable ones, are numbered. I don't like it." I stopped in my tracks as an idea came to me. "I'm going to launch a tree escape," I said. "I'll tear off the plaques!"

"You can't do that," Judy said.

"Go free brothers and sisters of the leaf!" I shouted, arms raised.

Judy looked at me gone mad.

"Freedom..." I trailed off. I was thinking about what branding had done. The Nazi regime branded Oma "Jew", my mother *Mischling*/half-breed and Rosa and Josef Skrainka, "*Lebensunwertes Leben*/Life unworthy of life". The branding was the beginning of the end.

Spires and chimneys finally appeared in the distance. Then came the revelation that our hotel was in the twin city to Schoenebeck called Salzelmen. We checked Constanze's notes for the day. Sure enough, we had another five kilometres to go from Schoenebeck to Salzelmen.

"I'm wringing lots out of my last full day of walking," Judy commented as we plodded along Schoenebeck's very long and busy main street. Judy was due to leave the day after Magdeburg. She had family obligations waiting for her in Canada.

We finally found our hotel. It was a handsome villa surrounded by gardens beside a small, artificial pond surrounded with beauteous flora and fauna. We had stumbled into the "hippest" little resort town we had yet seen, that was but for a large wooden contraption the size of a football field that we had spotted on our way into the burg.

"Well, I'm not far off with the humidifier theory," I said as I turned from research on my laptop. I had looked up the large, wooden contraption. "Deep in the earth below Salzelmen, there are salt and mineral deposits to cure what ails you. The contraption pulls the vapours up out of the earth. People come to take the waters by breathing them in and by bathing in them."

Judy and I went out to venture around the giant humidifier. We took in a heavy breath or two.

"Slightly salty tang," Judy said letting her tongue slide over her lips as if moisture had landed there.

"Hint of minerals," I said.

Judy laughed. "You'd think we were doing wine reviews!"

We walked around touristy Salzelmen and enjoyed its quaint ambience. It was not until my night-time reading that I realized an explosives plant, *Lignose Sprengstoff Werke GmbH*, was located on the outskirts of the twin cities of Schoenebeck-Salzelmen. It was the subject of U.S. strategic bombing at the end of WWII. The area had satellite camps for forced labour as elsewhere where there was a war industry. And although the small Jewish community was well respected, by the accounts that I read, its synagogue and Jewish graveyard fell to *Kristallnacht* violence.

I knew about the telegram that Reinhard Heydrich sent around the Greater German Reich with instructions on how to carry out the anti-Jewish measures of *Kristallnacht*, November 10, 1938. I had not read the response that the district manager of Schoenbeck sent to Heydrich, not until that night in Salzelmen.The district manager proudly related that nowhere did the NSDAP appear to be the instigator to the actions that caused damage. And yet, his thugs destroyed the inside of Schoenebeck's Moorish-styled synagogue and the Jewish cemetery. They vandalized five Jewish stores, searched 19 Jewish homes and sent ten Jewish men to the Buchenwald Concentration Camp. And, that happened to a small, respected Jewish community!

I lay back on my single bed in the lovely villa and my mind drifted to *Kristallnacht* in Vienna when Oma's parents had hidden in the shadows of their apartment. Josef and Rosa stayed in the shadows as Nazi hooligans smashed the showcase windows of their butcher store below; they could do nothing. Within days, the *Reich* ordered the Jews—

No, not "the Jews", I stopped myself. I hated that individuals were lumped together as "the Jews" or "the" anything. *The Reich ordered my great-grandfather Josef Skrainka* to make atonement payments. On November 14, 1938 the *Reichgesetzblatt*/government legislative gazette laid out that Jews had to pay a 20% tax on all their declared assets as of April 16, 1938. The "Atonement Fee" was for the damages of *Kristallnacht,* caused, not by Nazi hooligans, but instead by the actions of an agitated Jewish teenager who had shot a German diplomat in Paris on November 7, 1938. Yes, the scrawny 17-year-old Herschel Grynszpan was responsible for all of the damage!

It hadn't made sense then and it still didn't. Josef and Rosa Skrainka were law-abiding citizens with no need to atone. I felt *Kristallnacht* and the sheer unfairness of it and "atonement" as I lay in the villa in Schoenebeck-Salzelmen, 70 years after my great-grandparents hid in the shadows.

The next morning, a new, tall and portly driver arrived late at the villa. He was determined to make up for lost time with an effusive combination of travelogue and jokes. I was happy that Judy didn't understand his patter. I translated until he commented that he felt sorry for the Americans who had to choose between a woman and a "N——" to run for president. It was spring 2008; he meant Hillary Clinton and Barack Obama. He scoffed at the choice the Democratic Party of the U.S.A. had to make. He parked beside architect Friedensreich Hundertwasser's amorphous Green Citadel building in central Magdeburg to give us tourist information. He started with the sarcastic comment, "Look! In that entire building, that Jew Hundertwasser couldn't find one right-angle."

Judy knew something was wrong by the tone of my voice. I was terse in my request to drive immediately to our hotel. Later, after Judy and I discussed the driver's comments, we left a message for Constanze that we did not want to see the insufferable man again. Judy didn't need to worry. The next morning she had a taxi pickup to take her to Berlin for her flight home.

Judy and I went out to enjoy our last day together. Magdeburg was charming. We stumbled upon the *Frauenkloster*, an ancient nunnery that had been transformed into an art museum. As well as the marvels of the courtyard where we sat in a heaven-sent stony stillness, the museum had an eclectic collection that included fine, carved-wooden church decorations and a collection of supersize vases that sat and lay in the cloister's upstairs hallways like beached ceramic whales. The most modern gallery in the museum included audio-video installations.

I saw Judy ahead of me with headphones watching a video of what appeared to be a pleasant stroll along the Elbe, very similar to what we were doing. She recoiled all of a sudden, took off her headphones and came to get me. The video was on a loop. I put on the headphones and enjoyed the walk, when I too recoiled. Bang, BANG! I looked around me as if in the woods. BANG! Who was shooting? Where were they? Where could I hide? My reactions were involuntary.

"Do you think the video is about the hunting towers?" Judy asked as I took off the headphones.

"I think it goes back to Oma," I said. "Shots could have come from anywhere, during the war and after, when all the refugees were on the road."

"What would Oma have done if she'd heard shots?" Judy asked. The unnerving bangs made Judy and me stand closer in the darkened gallery.

"She probably ducked and cringed."

"We did," Judy said quietly, "just now."

We walked off into the sunlight and away from the shuddering realization of what it meant to be surrounded by the sounds of gunfire.

Decades after the post-war chaos, we wandered around totally rebuilt Magdeburg in search of its best ice cream establishment. We decided not to hold a grudge against the creamy ices and rich whipped cream because they had been recommended by our nasty driver. We sat on an outdoor sidewalk patio soaking up the hot spring sun, tempting sunburn.

We patronized a classy restaurant that evening, dressed in the best clothes we could muster. We reminisced. Between the Elbe walk and the walk around Lake Ontario, Judy and I had shared 1500 kilometres of adventure. We were a walking, talking, feeling machine. I was fortunate to have a friend with whom I finally shared my ambivalence about Germany and my mother. It had helped to talk my jumbled feelings through with a "Guidance Counsellor".

I still had a long way to go before Hamburg, but Judy and I had captured a great deal about Oma's trek along the Elbe. I was also starting to see my mother in a new light. I was not sure that the trek would yield more. In many ways I felt the trip was over.

Chapter Sixteen: The Universe Hums

Judy's taxi stood in front of the hotel turned towards Berlin. Her suitcase and backpack were wedged in. I have never been one to hug much. My mother's short fuse saw to that. I never knew if I could go to her for comfort or if it was better to run and hide. But Judy. I gave her a big hug.

"I hate to leave you..." Judy said. She trailed off to wipe moist eyes.

"I'll be careful," I said. I stood dressed and ready for my first solo day. "See, I have everything: water, Constanze's map with directions, rain gear."

Judy wept outright as the taxi pulled away. My eyes filled too. I had already started to miss her the night before while we were at supper and later as she slept.

Although David had returned to Prague and was staying with Robbie, I would not see him for a few days yet. He would spend time in Prague before using Robbie's car to meet me in Tangermuende. Robbie took a paternal interest in David whom he had known for 40 years. They would pal around and likely discuss everything from tire gauges to Reinhard Heydrich's assassination in Prague, not ever touching on anything remotely personal. That was their way.

I thought about the many personal things Judy and I shared. We grew into one another with the sharing. A voice in my head suddenly interrupted with: *Time to go!* With Judy's taxi long gone, I had to start the walk, alone for the first time.

I had planned to take a bus to the Magdeburg Water Bridge at Hohenwarth and then walk back to Magdeburg. I was intrigued by the canal that allowed large ships to navigate over the Elbe. On our walk around Lake Ontario, Judy and I had seen that the Erie Canal was built over a small local stream. That was impressive. This canal over a huge river had to be grander. Back in Magdeburg, I would tour Hundertwasser's Green Citadel building complex. I had plotted all the required connections.

"Send out the hounds if I'm not back by 7PM," I said to the ladies at the hotel desk. The nice desk ladies smiled. They thought I was joking, but I wasn't.

I noted significant features of the landscape, but then I also noted a new voice. It started talking to me on the bus to Hohenwarth.

Read the architecture, it said. *Note what it tells you.*

I saw lots of church spires and industrial smoke stacks. They represented the ebb and flow of industrial and spiritual hope.

Focus on the details, the voice interrupted. *They will help you get back to the hotel.*

The bus arrived in the small hamlet of Hohenwarth where it stopped in front of, yes, a bakery! The voice in my head cut in snidely: *Get in a little walking before you stop for a treat.*

I obediently headed down the narrow lane the bus driver said led to the Elbe Canal Bridge. I had taken only a few paces when I froze. The stork ahead on a chimney preened with the sun perfectly positioned. That had to be the best stork photo ever! I set my Elbe map book on top of one of the lane's high brick walls to grab my camera. To my horror, the book plummeted off the top, over to the far side of the wall. I heard its invisible plop.

My god, the book is in someone's back yard! Look over the wall! See whose house is connected to the wall where the book fell. You're helpless without that book. You'll never make it back.

While the voice raged, I tried to gather myself, to be calm, to think.

You're on your own but a few hours and look what you've done. How will you manage on your own?

Somehow with the jibber-jabber in my head, I figured out which house probably had my book in its yard. I rang the bell, twice. No answer. I hoped to avoid another Pirna Criminal Police incident that on this occasion would feature my apprehension by the Hohenwarth constabulary in a widow's vegetable patch. I went back across the street to the bakery to get help.

I spat out my tale of woe to the stunned disbelief of the bakery woman. I saw her mull over just how crazy I was. My *Deutschland* police dossier thickened. All of a sudden a cognition switch went on in the lady's eyes.

She shouted back through a door to an unseen person. "Mother, mind the store," and off she dashed across the street with the straps of her baker's apron flying in her wake.

"Anneliese, open up." Pause. "Anneliese, open up!" Then a lot louder, " Anneliese!" the counter lady shouted.

I was sure Anneliese cowered behind the lace curtains. After all, a stranger had rung her doorbell, twice. The third shout did the trick. With the bakery lady to give her strength, Anneliese opened her castle's keep. The ladies headed to the back of her garden. I leaned into the gateway, but dared not intrude. I saw my book lifted out of the red-leafed lettuce.

Well, there's the proof you're not a mad laneway woman shaking down German widows, the voice said.

Even with the book in hand, the duo stared at me from the back of the garden. They whispered back and forth.

They still think something is amiss, the voice speculated.

I remained standing politely outside the gate and as the minutes ticked on, the duo's doubts resolved. I purchased a coffee and rhubarb strudel back at the bakery, out of gratitude. Then I headed to the fateful lane way.

"Damn you!" I said to the stork's pinhead, now only slightly protruding from its stick nest. I passed it with a huge huff. It seemed that not all storks were good luck after all!

I threaded my way through Hohenwarth's pleasant streets and found the canal. It was amazing that the structure bore the weight of all that water and of huge ships too. Although the canal was not totally filled for the new shipping season, a boat that waited outside the canal's gate gave a sense of scale for the grand undertaking.

It has been worth the trip said the voice now recovered from the guidebook fiasco. But, the voice was not done with command. It added: *Now that you don't have Judy to talk, talk, talk, listen to the silence.*

I tuned my antennae. The sounds of industry and traffic predominated for a while. These drowned out the birdsong in the groves of flowering bushes that filled the small space between the houses and the river. The narrow path widened out near an abandoned building. A sand hill was to my left. The hill morphed into ochre-coloured sand cliffs laced with holes for birds' nests. Finally, there were no longer any man-made sounds when I made it to a small wood. I enjoyed the walk accompanied by birdsong until the mechanical sound of a chugging motor indicated an unseen boat beyond the curtain of trees. Judging by the motor's grunting, the boat fought its way upstream against the Elbe's currents.

The hills and cliffs gave way to Elbe flatlands that continued on for kilometres. I was walking through ancient Elbe meanders. The Elbe's twists and turns were writ large. The sun was out, not a tree was in sight and the path was now busy with cyclists. I discovered that long, hot kilometres without conversation, and a full bladder, prompted the speculative mind.

I started to wonder how wide a sapling had to be to constitute cover for a washroom break. And, why bicycle paths were longer than the way crows fly? Why did shapes morph into something else when you got closer to them? Rolls of hay I had spotted from afar turned out to be sheep grazing. The dog I had imagined was instead a log sticking out of a field. A small gathering of bushes that was seemingly ideal for a washroom break—well, it wasn't.

I could not say if it was the absence of Judy, or urea poisoning, that led to my first sheep conversation. The sheep nestled into bushes for shade called out, as if to me personally as I walked along the electric fence of a large sheep enclosure. I made a few tentative *baas* in response to their invitations and to my surprise I received *baas* in answer. I thought I might be imagining things, but then very quickly I was engrossed in a sheep dialogue. I varied my *baas*, and commensurate *baas* come back in reply. I had never been this at-one with sheep. As I passed the last paddock,

I sent farewell *baas* back to my sheep friends, to which I heard a chorus of replies in the distance. My imagination? Hell, no.

I had another strange experience a thousand or so more flat fields along. I was proceeding towards high-power lines that stretched over the Elbe when I heard an unearthly sound. What was it? The voice in my head, that had been quiet for a while, went into overdrive.

Monkey screeches? Singing handsaws? Whale song?

That didn't seem right. It had to be something scientific. Okay, I thought, just as planets lined up in a particular way for eclipses, the wind and high voltage electricity wires on those transmission towers had aligned to make the humming sound. Yes, that was it. Singing wires. I was satisfied. The voice wasn't.

Is the universe coming unglued? It scoffed. *Or you?*

Now that was cheeky! I stopped in my tracks under the towers. The negativity in the voice triggered epiphany. I had been on my own only for a short time, but I had a niggling, negative voice that walked with me. Where had I heard that before?

"Welcome, mommy dearest!" I said out loud and laughed. I should have known. My mother had awaited her chance. She had jumped into the silence left by Judy's absence. Her small voice came to me with the freight of its trauma. Thanks, but no thanks!

Judy was fun. My mother's WWII experiences left her emotionally scarred and paranoid. I did not need her ability to see the worst, to insinuate her biases, to doubt me and yet at the same time to overprotect me. I had grown up with that and thanks to the walk, I realized I still had emotional baggage to divest.

I calculated the time difference with Canada and dialed the little cherub Oma dandled back in 1972. Our daughter, Jennifer, picked up before the third ring. We carried on a conversation as if we were the few kilometres apart that our houses are in Toronto; it felt good. Judy was in the skies above me; David was on the highway headed towards me and our daughter tended the home fires. All was right with my world. I had worked very hard to be a mother different from the one I had experienced. Mostly, I'd done it. I could do better still.

I hung up and said out loud, "Okay, mother, if you're coming along, we will look for the good in what we see." I wasn't sure that comment would work but at least I knew what was going on. I trudged ahead looking for the Elbe crossover bridge.

Finally, I saw a public washroom kiosk. Rescued! I relieved my overburdened bladder but then had to quick-step past Magdeburg's historic town walls, castles and churches to make it on time for the architecture tour of the Green Citadel. A knowledgeable young art historian toured us around the pink building, into its basement and up to an empty flat near the top. I understood more about Hundertwasser's experience as a *Mischling*/half-breed as the guide spoke about the building's undulating structure and recycled materials. Hundertwasser had associated straight lines, fastidious counting and obsessive record-keeping with fascism and Nazis.

I was gleeful. I understood the rejection of rigorous, nigh on fascistic order. It was not right to brand trees and certainly not humans. I smiled as I talked to the spirit of the building. Every detail in the sprawling, irregular design spoke to me about freedom, including the fact that Hundertwasser allowed the artisans a free hand to create their own designs as they experimented with recycled materials. Hundertwasser insisted that even the underground parking spots be unnumbered. Way to go, Hundertwasser!

I thought about what my mother might build if she were an architect. She was a *Mischling* like Hundertwasser. A small suburban bungalow in Whitby, Ontario, took shape in my mind. It grew upwards into the impenetrable tower my mother created to lock me up, her own Rapunzel. "Trust no one!" kept sounding in my ears. I shook away the vision and started to walk along the sprawling, pink, outer facade of the citadel, in the direction of my hotel.

That first night alone in Magdeburg I searched for articles on Intergenerational trauma. At first I only wanted to know why Hundertwasser and my mother reacted differently. Then I couldn't stop reading. I had instinctively known, even as a teenager, that a total meltdown over shoes not lined up properly was wrong. I read long into the night as it slowly sunk in that Oma, my mother and me were variations on the effects of trauma. At least one of the characteristic reactions of trauma survivors was that they used their own child as a "container" for the negative emotions they couldn't express. I latched onto that characteristic. It explained my mother's actions towards me in a way that I could see them as misdirected rather than intentional.

The next day, I made the 11:09 morning train to Rogaetz. It sped through the rain-splattered countryside and quickly reached Angern, the start point for the walk plotted by Constanze.

"Madam, this is your stop," the conductor confirmed as she looked at my ticket. I hesitated at the unlikelihood. There was no river anywhere, but, I got off. The station lady pointed me in the direction of the Elbe ferry. I plodded ahead through an uninspiring stretch of farm, industrial and residential lands. A putrid, yellow mountain of sulphur, like those I'd seen in Canada's oil sands in northern Alberta, sat inside a tall, wooden fence; its sulphurous presence dominated the landscape.

The village of Rogaetz, ahead, featured ornate houses and single-storied, cross-beamed cottages. The picturesque houses had sunk below street level over the centuries. They looked as if they might disappear totally with time. The drab surrounding country would swallow them. Gulp. Gone. Why not an ancient village gone in a gulp? Things disappeared. I was thinking specifically of the Czech village of Lidice, razed to the ground by the Nazis in reprisal for the killing of Reinhard Heydrich in 1942. Goya's painting *Saturn Devouring his Son,* came to mind as well. Walking brought waves of images, ideas and insights.

The ferry crossing just beyond Rogaetz had about ten cars in a queue; the drivers stood chatting. I was by myself at the side of the river. After a very quick crossing, the cars and vans shot off the ferry and were quickly gone. I walked among fields flowering bright yellow with canola, the same yellow as the sulphur heap. I turned back to look towards Rogaetz' medieval silhouette nestled against colourful fields; it was prettier in passing.

The dyke ahead was wide, paved, and bathed in full sunshine. I walked along in sublime pastoral beauty until I noticed a huge bird's nest in nearby woods. It could not be a stork's nest by its lofty location. What huge bird would set up residence in a small wood?

I continued on, past pleasant pastures. I saw towers eventually. The city of Burg was famous for its towers. I wanted to see the *Hexen Turm*/Witches' Tower I had read about. The guide book entry said that in medieval times "rowdy girls" were punished there. I felt that something had gone wrong in translation. What happened to witches went well beyond what was appropriate for the punishment for rowdy girls. I was pondering my favourite theme of disproportionate punishment, when my mother's voice tuned in again.

Yes, you'd fit in alright, with rowdy women, the voice piped up. *And, Oma would too.*

My mother was correct about that. Oma and I would have been locked in the tower for various offenses. My mother, on the other hand, would tidy the tower and look around to see if anyone was watching to tell her that she was doing a good job. Trauma had made very different women of Oma, my mother and me. I'd seen that in my readings the night before.

But, look at the time. You've got to get a move on, my mother's voice interrupted.

I looked at my watch and picked up my pace, which was difficult as I was in the area of Burg's Crisp Bread factory. What a heavenly aroma! The whole world smelled of things baking. I was taken right back to the smells and sights of the kitchen in our Hamburg apartment where the dough my mother kneaded sat on the counter for the yeast to rise, and where sandy-coloured bread came out of the wood-burning oven.

If you don't make it to Parey to connect with your new driver, you're scuppered, the irritated voice said.

I would make the rendezvous I thought, but I became uncertain when I looked at the sun's passage in the sky. I convinced myself that all would go well while my mother's voice drifted in and out doing its negative schtick as it had done all my life. There would be no time for the witches' tower.

I sat on an outdoor bench with a young woman at Guesen. She waited for the same bus I was to take. I asked her so many questions that she took me under wing. We were the only two on board when we eventually got on the bus for Parey. She and I studied Constanze's map for the day. The young lady had not heard of a train station in Parey and she lived there.

"There has to be an old train station somewhere," I said several different ways in case I was saying something wrong in German. The various bus stops ticked away like minutes towards midnight. We would soon be out of Parey proper. Suddenly the bus made an abrupt halt.

"Out, out now!" the bus driver shouted into the mirror. He glared at me.

I looked out the window of the bus. There was neither a bus stop nor a train station. The driver flung open the door of the bus with a clatter and gestured to the outside with great force.

"Go! There! Go!" He pointed at an inauspicious subdivision street. He was very agitated because he had halted between stops. I gathered my stuff and got off. The door closed; the bus sped off.

You've done it now! You're headed down a street that has nothing to do with train stations in a town you don't know, in the middle of Germany and it's raining. What is the matter with you? Why did you get off the bus? How will you get to Tangermuende now? Face it, you're doomed.

I began to think my mother was right. There were no indicators it would work out. Maybe I had become too much a risk-taker as on over-reaction to my mother's mistrust of the world. I walked down the residential street through the drizzle going heaven knows where, wondering what my next steps should be when the road turned out to be a dead end. Then the road widened a little about a block on. I saw train tracks way ahead in that extra space.

Still not a train station, is it?

Nevertheless, the tracks gave me hope. I believed in the powers I had developed to deal with vicissitudes. My career in education had played to my problem-solving strengths and developed them further. Then like magic, on the other side of the tracks, I spotted a lone taxi. I strode towards the vehicle not knowing what to expect; the driver advanced towards me. We both paused. It was the showdown at the OK Corral.

"Mrs. Littlefield?" the casually dressed man asked at the three-pace mark.

I nodded; we stepped closer; we shook hands. Then we both laughed. We bent over with great belly laughs. How was it possible that two people had arrived from different locations and had both found a non-existent train station? For there was none. As the driver pointed to the foundation stones resting under the grass nearby, his phone rang. It was a very worried Constanze. The new driver, Herr Joerg Puetsch, had notified her that the rendezvous point to which we were both directed, no longer existed. He had found the site of the former station by asking around.

I overheard Constanze ask, "Any sign of Mrs. Littlefield?" I sensed her concern. It was hard to explain losing a client in the middle of Germany.

Fortunately the bus driver, who had eavesdropped on the young lady's and my conversation, had broken protocol to stop the bus to send me to the ghost train station he knew about. Fortunately I got off, and fortunately, the cab driver used his considerable detective skills. What serendipity! A great start for my new driver Herr Puetsch.

We chatted and laughed like old buddies on the scenic drive to Tangermuende. He told me about the street fighting and the tanks that went through Tangermuende at war's end. He drove me to the location of the former bridge, blown up by the Germans April 12, 1945. My first view of Tangermuende was from the perspective of the east side of the exploded bridge where long columns of refugees had been frantic as Russians approached behind them. The Russian's reputation for revenge and rape preceded them. With the bridge gone, the refugees had no way across. To worsen that fear, retreating Germans were shooting anyone not seen to defend the Reich.

Despair rose from the very sand where Herr Puetsch and I stood. I felt its faint vibrations; Oma had lived through it. Then we crossed the river and drove through the walls of the ancient town. Herr Puetsch stopped for me to buy a book that he recommended about the last days of the war in Tangermuende. The book would make good reading as I waited for David.

I greeted Herr Puetsch the next morning with details from the book. He was pleased. We quickly got out of the way that I was no fanatic about walking every centimetre from Theresienstadt to Hamburg, especially as I knew Oma had sped past stretches with rides into which she'd charmed her way. With that in mind, we picked Schelldorf as my day's start point.

We headed off in the direction of Bittkau. Herr Puetsch pointed out the rise of land that zealous officer trainees from Potsdam used as their last stand for Tangermuende at the end of WWII. We drove past rows of hillocks where we saw Polish guest workers harvest the white asparagus Germans prize. I saw the Peutsch's lovely homestead. In Grieben, we visited a rebuilt, old-style, wooden windmill. The mill volunteer was proud to show us the oven where she had just baked the bread whose wonderful aroma hung on the crisp morning air. She opened the semicircular hole in the wall and reached in with a flat wooden implement to slide out a new loaf.

Don't even think it, I said to my mother's voice. I knew she wanted to chime in.

Can you blame me? That oven is a mini-crematorium.

It did look like one, but I forced my attention to my day's walk. Herr Puetsch gave me a gift bottle of beer as I was about to head off. How nice was that! I seized the beer with thanks and headed down long, lovely country roads where every view was worthy of a photo: a wagon with hay set against a flowering stand of bushes, a rivulet with muddy banks backing onto the colourful rising gardens of the cottages of the hamlet, Buch. All beautiful.

An open door into a courtyard seduced me at Buch's crossroads. I wanted to penetrate this enclosed world because the closed doors of ancient farm courtyards, up to this point, had excluded me. The open door of the local museum housed in a *Bauernhof,* or farmer's complex, provided a fantastic excuse to snoop. The layout of the roomy courtyard and the displays of farm equipment in the adjoining buildings were the stimulation I needed to imagine the busy life of every barnyard I had passed. I could imagine the refuge that weary travelers more than 60 years before could have found in such places. I watched a video on banding eagles as an added bonus. Aha, the large nest from the day before had been an eagle's aerie.

I made my way along more country roads during the peak of the noonday sun. I wanted to drink Herr Puetsch's beer, but alas, I had no opener and it was not a screw top. I scrutinized bicycle riders to determine if I could ask for a bottle opener. No one looked receptive to being flagged down by a lone pedestrian desperate for a bottle opener. On top of that, there would be no end to the chiding from mommy if I spoke to strangers. Time to be inventive, I thought. I saw a dyke starting in the distance. It was sure to have a metal gate to keep out cars from the road below it. With all the metal angles on the gate there had to be one to relieve a beer bottle of its cap. My first few experiments failed but I was rewarded when the right angle caused a sudden splash of beer. That *worsteln*/fiddling my father talked about had paid off once again.

I clambered up the dyke where a breathtaking wetland vista awaited. Trees were reflected in the water; ducks called to one another; birds zigzagged overhead. I sat down by the still waters with my bottle of beer, munched some nuts and savoured the moment.

Tangermuende soon announced itself with a row of double trees called an allee not long after my peaceful, beer interlude. There were anglers on the river, cyclists on the path and pedestrians on a Saturday outing. I proceeded into Tangermuende to coffee and cake at the Post Restaurant. I went next to rest on the bench in front of the church on the main square. I had read the whole book on the last days of the war by the time the sun's heat waned. I pictured the street fighting and panzers. I sat among burned and shelled buildings and pitted roadways where lives were lost. In 1945, the allee I had just walked had been crammed with locals fleeing the fighting.

I walked to the hotel to prepare for the arrival of my beloved. It had been a month since I left our home in Canada. I wondered if he would see some of the changes that I already felt in myself. Would his powers of observation see my mother's negative grasp loosening?

I knew for sure that David's penchant for organization would colour the rest of the experience, but how? I awaited what the morrow would bring.

Chapter Seventeen: The Showdown at Gross Ellingen

David arrived in good humour. He had made stops in Torgau and Magdeburg to visit places I had recommended. We caught up over supper and agreed that everything would go according to the routines I had established, except the daily sharing would come at the end of my solo walking. David was not used to walking distances and especially not at my pace. He would explore in a leisurely way during the day with Robbie's car.

The next morning we parted ways after a pleasant breakfast. I started along Lange Street, formerly *Adolf Hitler Strasse.* David was going to tool around Tangermuende until Herr Puetsch picked me up at Storkau. We would take the Grete Minden tour after that. Grete's story was from 1619 when she had been falsely accused of setting the town on fire and then burned at the stake. The tour promised to divert us from the pervasive presence of WWII imprinted in the very stones of Tangermuende.

The way to the Elbe path led me through industrial lands. A plaque told me that a huge complex of buildings, that now sold used DDR army clothes and equipment, was once the property of a former chocolate king. In the hectic final war days of 1945, rival armies and inhabitants alike looted Meyers' Chocolate Factory. Blocks of chocolate, cocoa oil and fats flowed into all hands.

I passed an opulent villa, a former Meyer residence. Friedrich Hugo Ernst Meyer, son of an old-time Caribbean "sugar king", withdrew to Hamburg after WWII to continue chocolate-making with his new Fedora brand, of which I had enjoyed more than a few samples. Passing the Meyer villa stirred memories of my mother and I sharing chocolate confections at our

Stammtisch/regular meeting spot in Hamburg. How nice it was to rediscover good times when there was conversation and laughter with my mother.

I saw a widely spanned bridge and the bicycle path not long after I was past the Meyer complex. The sun headed towards burn intensity as I walked through wide Elbe meadows called *Auen*. The first break in the routine of nodding politely to weekend bicycle and pedestrian traffic came as I approached the small hamlet of Haemerten. I heard strange sounds. A large wetland lay before me. I looked around. No electricity wires. I ventured towards the shallow water filled to the brim with vibrating reeds from whence came the sounds.

"Come out, come out, whatever you are," I cooed. "I know you're in there."

I could not see them, but I suspected the strange harmonies were frogs. With my camera poised to reveal the mystery, just as I reached any particular area on the edge of the pond, the sounds stopped. Frog music/step/silence/frog music/step/silence.

"We're scoring a frog sonata, are we?" I said to the choir.

I walked away from the pond with slightly soggy feet and without a photo. Behind my back, the music rose into a resounding finale with just a tinge of mockery to underscore it.

The road morphed into a country lane once I was through Haemerten. Bushes in bloom mostly blocked the views of fields on both sides. Small birds darted in and out of the hedges and swooped overhead. There was a railroad underpass in the middle of this long stretch of bucolic landscape. The deserted railroad station to its right stood by tracks that led to a distant, black-metal bridge over the Elbe. A memorial for the German lads who had died defending the bridge greeted me on the far side of the underpass. *"Et tu Brute,"* I said to the plaque. The war followed me even into the quiet, deserted countryside.

I was almost in Storkau at this point, well before the rendezvous time. Organ music drifted out of the tiny, red-brick church where I was to meet Herr Puetsch. I read on the church's announcement board that I had arrived on one of the few Sundays when this small evangelical church had a service.

I took off my camera and Canada cap and slipped into a cool rear pew. Five people attended the service earnestly conducted by a young minister. A beatifically smiling lady walked towards me and handed me a hymn book. I followed the German service, mouthing the words to *The Lord's Prayer* in English. Every once in a while the minister fumbled with buttons on a tape recorder and we seven launched into robust song.

The minister referred to false gods during his sermon about the power of prayer. When he pointed out that the prayer, "Please Lord, give me a handy," was inappropriate, I froze. I had a "handy". That was what the Germans called the cell phone my friend Ludwig loaned me. I surreptitiously took it out of my pocket. I was new to cell phones. I did not know how to shut it off. I could charge it, yes. Turn it off, no.

I was sure imminent ringing would damn me to hell when canned organ music started again. I ran outside and stuck Mammon's "handy" behind a gravestone, then I re-entered singing so as not to arouse suspicion. I had pulled it off. While the minister concentrated on conversation with his sparse flock, I swept the phone up from the care of one of Storkau's long-deceased and hurriedly ran outside the church walls. I had escaped damnation, for a while at least.

Herr Puetsch arrived shortly thereafter and spirited me back to Tangermuende. The Grete Minden tour took David and me to all corners of the old town. We ended at a lookout tower that had a panoramic views of city and countryside. About three floors up the spiraling wooden staircase of this tower, we confronted life-sized, emaciated, carved wooden figures. Caught in the sunlight from the window behind them, the shivering forms reminded me of holocaust victims.

"That's not what they are," countered David. "Here, take a photo of me." With that, David picked a wooden buddy and threw his arm around him. Ah, to be like David, I thought and Renate and Ludwig Hendricks. WWII did not touch them as it did me.

I knew objectively that German war guilt should not attach to me and yet I still had to cut the emotional ties to it in the same way as I had to exorcise the damage of my mother's tantrums. It was time. She had not shouted at me for eight years since her death.

The next day was my last with Herr Puetsch. We detoured to the house of one of his friends on the way to the day's start. There, sitting in a front yard as if planted, was a MIG-21 fighter plane from DDR times. I looked up and down the street. It was a normal residential scene. Only this plane before me was no butterfly bush. I speculated that Herr Puetsch's friend was a former DDR pilot who had overcome separation anxiety by letting his plane move in. Imagine bringing that home!

"Honey, I'd like you to meet Miggy. She's going to stay with us for a while"

I snapped photos as I knew Robbie would have plane envy as soon as he heard about this. I read up on the MIG-21 before I emailed the photo. The Soviet supersonic jet fighter, fast, agile, dependable and easy to maintain, was everything a WWII flyboy like Robbie liked. He, who had flown Lancasters, Corsairs and Wellingtons, would appreciate the slick, compact, dog-fighting MIG-21. I already imagined the phone call.

Just north of Arneburg, Herr Puetsch set me on a scenic tree-lined highway to start another day of walking. I had admired so much of Germany's natural beauty by this point that I played games with it for new camera shots. I started to look at the scenery as planes of colour. I understood what Van Gogh saw in the fields near Arles. Here, the dark green forest contrasted beautifully with the bright yellow canola fields in the foreground and dotted among them were strong dark lines, trees in flower. Just then, a train loaded with thick logs chugged into the view in the distance. Painterly!

The fields led to a forest and eventually I crossed the rail line which I had seen in the distance just a short while before. I was headed towards Gross Ellingen. With muscled legs pumping and lots of time on my hands, I ruminated about the ants that undermined the interlocking bricks of the bike path. That led to thoughts about the mouse holes I had seen in the dykes.

Good grief, you're thinking about ants and mice! Get a grip.

There it was again. Mommy dearest never totally disappeared.

A huge covered storage area heaped with round golden bales of hay heaved into view about then. It immediately diverted me with a great photo opportunity. A mountain of gold set against a clear blue sky. I grabbed my camera from around my neck. That was when I spotted them. A herd of about 15 cows had escaped from somewhere. I knew this because I could see that there was no fence between the youthful escapees and myself. Nevertheless, I advanced into the field to take photos.

I must have piqued the interest of the rebel herd as they started moving towards me. Great, I thought, as I framed them in my viewfinder. Their red phalanx was set against a large expanse of green. Great contrast. Then I noticed they had stopped their advance. I looked up to see that behind them, even further in the distance, their herders were trying to catch up with them. I looked behind me. I was all that lay between the heifers and freedom.

I first became anxious when I heard snorts. Hooves scratched the earth and heads wagged up and down. I recognized a challenge from my years of dealing with teenagers as a vice-principal and principal. There was fire in them-there red-rimmed eyes. They were coming for me and I could not outrun them. Before the bovine advance got any further, I used my best principal voice, raised my arm, and shouted, "Stay!"

The cows recognized authority. They halted the pawing, looked again towards me and then back to the approaching herders and off they went in a wild dash, arcing around me towards the bike path in the direction from whence I had just come. I caught my breath as 15 cows, spraying saliva, narrowly booted it by me down the bike path with a mini-car in hot pursuit. I had survived the showdown at Gross Ellingen!

I calmed my nerves not long after by ordering a *Bockwurst* in a local eatery. I practically burst into song when I smelled the sizzling meat. I reminisced happily about all the *knacked* or burst sausages I had consumed over the years. I studied Constanze's maps during this relaxing and savoury snack break. But, I was puzzled. None of the community names past Gross Ellingen matched anything in the book.

Aren't you concerned? my mother's voice asked.

Well, I was but I sure as hell was not giving in to the fears her voice represented.

At the crossroads back in Hindenburg, not one town name on the signpost, in any direction, matched your book. Who knows where we're going?

I walked on with my usual bravado, but when I saw a gnome-like man leaning over a fence at a crossroad, I decided to consult him. He had a collection of bicycles set up by his fence; he told me he was trying to sell them. When he determined I would not buy, he mumbled and pointed in the direction I thought I should go.

How do you know he's not the Lorelei of the bike path? Look at all the bicycles he has. He's lured cyclists to their deaths.

I ignored my mother's voice again and went with the old man's directions. I hoped not to be dashed on the rocks onto which the Lorelei lured sailors. My mother knew that I loved the Lorelei song about sirens. She stopped at nothing to get me to be fearful. Just because she saw betrayal everywhere, did not mean I had to. I'd known that fact as a teen; I knew it even better now after nights of reading up on post-traumatic stress disorder/PTSD. My mother's nerves were always shot and she showed other PTSD symptoms. I stomped ahead. I finally felt I might be going in the right direction when I reached Schwarzholz.

See the Elbe anywhere? There's not even a hint of the river.

True. There had not been any hint of the river for many kilometres. I passed only fields split by sludge-filled irrigation ditches. These ditches reminded me of the child's chant: *Hoppe, Hoppe Reiter/Hop, Hop, Rider.* I had dandled baby Jennifer up and down on my lap to lyrics that talked about a rider falling into a ditch only to face the danger of being eaten by ravens—that nice German humour for children! These murky sloughs before me were those very ditches. I loved them!

As I walked, I heard my great-grandmother Rosa chant to Oma, she to my mother, my mother to me and then I to

Jennifer. The rhyme always ended with a dip backwards and—*PLUMPS!!* My mother, like those before her, had tried for childish squeals of delight and laughter with me. She had her lighter moments. One Christmas she had joined happily into the outrageous pantomime I'd devised. She cheerily played her assigned role of all three wise men rolled into one. Uncle Willy, the former dadaist, protested his role as "the ass".

I had been amazed when Jennifer sounded out the Hoppe-Hoppe rhyme to her two babies when they came along. I heard their shrieks of glee that had, for generations, followed at the backwards dip on "Plumps". Black birds suddenly rose into the air before me. Ravens, just like in the the rhyme. I smiled. The loud caws softened into the distance. The past could be magical. I needed to look for more of its good moments.

I retraced my steps a few times, but finally, when I hit Rittergut, I saw I was on target. From then on it was a progress through farmers' fields with only a few deviations. There was a plaque for one of Napoleon's battles, and a signed ecosystem from whence frogs once again sang to me. I smelled the end to the day's walk when I reached Butterhoff. Home stretch ahead!

I settled down at a scenic restaurant to wait. That was when I received my second surprise for the day when Herr Puetsch pulled up with his wife. Her family had been fleeing Sudeten-Germans at the time Oma walked along the Elbe. We shared beers and stories in the wonderful warm sun on the restaurant's patio.

Frau Puetsch told me that her parents had seen concentration camp survivors among the Sudetens who made their way north in 1945. The road conditions were harsh and dangerous, but among the displaced there was sharing. Frau Puetsch's stories were the perfect ending to the chapter that had started at the phantom train station in Parey. Herr Puetsch and I chuckled over that chance meeting as we hugged good-bye.

I was changing. I loved the hugging and was beginning to look at my past differently.

Chapter Eighteen: The Hero of the Havel

The next day David and I drove to Wittenberge where Constanze had arranged for more period witnesses. Reporters were in the mix. We met two lady reporters right away in the hotel's restaurant and I was delighted by their interest in the Oma project. One of them knew a teacher who had worked with students to erect a memorial for forced labourers at a camp called Gloewen near Nitzow. She promised to get in touch with the woman for the following evening interviews in Ruehstaedt.

The next morning I awaited a new driver outside Hotel Prignitz on the inauspicious, East-German Bismarck Square of Wittenberge. He was late. I used Ludwig's handy to find out why. There had been a miscue and the driver's wife was hastily pressed into service. She arrived and set about trying to find the day's start point.

As fate would have it, Robbie called to check on me just as we reached what I thought would be the start of a short cut. There was no sign of the path, but I didn't want to keep the tense lady driver waiting. I waved her off and started to walk while still talking with Robbie. After the call, I saw from double-checking that I'd gone the wrong way. I was in an orderly suburban stretch called Nitzow.

And here it came.

You just had to jump out, didn't you? Never think ahead. Now look. You're six kilometres out of the way and if you go back it's worse!

What could I say? I should have been more careful. Mommy dearest was not always wrong. I picked up my pace. To get to Ruehstaedt for 1PM I needed to walk faster. I speed-walked through a forested military area sealed behind barbed wire. There were many notices warning of dangers, but, no worries, mother was on task.

Look at the signs. This area is used for shooting practice. Keep your head down.

I could probably have out-sped bullets at the rate I was going.

Joke now, but, we'll talk in five kilometres!

I stopped my quick pace when I saw a memorial ahead. Was this the memorial at Gloewen about which the reporter spoke? I crossed the road to read the plaque and sure enough, it was. I took photos. Then after a few right-angle turns down long roads without any sign of the Elbe, forests turned to fields and finally, a river appeared.

Is it the Elbe or the Havel? Admit it, you don't know. We're still lost. Again, that trepidation.

I knew exactly where I was when I saw both rivers together. I put my finger on the point in the map book.

Well maybe you're back on track, but you'll never make it to Ruehstaedt for 1 PM.

I checked my watch. Indeed, I could not make it. I phoned my lady driver and changed the pickup to Abbendorf at 1:30. I relaxed the pace to enjoy the astounding beauty of a walk with two rivers within view. I had started in a hilly, forested area in the morning, but I was now on a spit of land between two rivers. The Elbe was a full-flowing river on which I saw the occasional cargo ship, whereas the Havel was a lush wetland with ducks, storks, swans and smaller birds.

I marveled at the first blooming lilac of the trip. The dark mauve flowers decorated an anglers' club on the spit. I had not seen any people for quite a while and enjoyed the scenic walk. Things continued in this idyllic fashion until I noticed bicycle riders on the far shore of the Havel. Hmm. There was a bicycle path over there too? That gave me pause. The Havel was now a full river between me and Abbendorf.

The sign at the beginning of the spit had said "Bicycle Path to Ruehstaedt". Did I have to go all the way to Ruehstaedt to cross the Havel River? My heart sank. That would mean many more kilometres than planned. I ignored the truth for a while, but as the Havel widened further with no bridge in sight, I knew I would have to go all the way to Ruehstaedt and then double back to Abbendorf.

You'll never make it. It's going on 1 PM now, and there's an extra six kilometres beyond what you reckoned. The driver is probably on the way to Abbendorf.

Reassuring as always! I picked up the pace. I strode at such a great speed that I felt shin splints coming on. Sweat streamed down my back and rivulets down my face. These were strange phenomena for me as I rarely sweated. While I maniacally considered swimming across the Havel, I spotted him. Way up ahead was a small boat with a fisherman in it. The man sported a bright orange raincoat. An idea came to me as I closed in on the distance between the man in the boat and myself. I was going to flag him down.

Flag down a stranger. Are you crazy? You can't just flag down a strange man in a boat.

I checked my watch. It was 1:30. Driven by desperation and dripping with sweat from sustained effort, I ran down the slope towards the marshy shoreline of the Havel River.

"Hello, hello! Over here!" I waved my arms excitedly. The man didn't hear what I said but he sensed my anguish.

"Wait there," he yelled back, as he pulled stuff up into his boat and started towards me.

I was so excited I had a boat ride, and near Abbendorf too, that I rushed into the Havel.

"Slow down," yelled the hero of the Havel, "I'm coming to you."

Once in the small boat, I blurted out my story as we headed to the far shore. The kind man smiled indulgently. He was not an old man, but he had the patience of a grandfather. I offered to pay him, but I knew my rescuer was a good Samaritan.

He waved and I hurried off on the final lap to Abbendorf. This little craft that had magically appeared to take me across the Havel was the first small boat I'd seen on the whole journey. I felt I had walked on water. I had an inexplicable sense that no matter how far I went wrong, there was someone watching over me and a sure way forward. I had always thought it was Oma but then, it was my mother who kept talking to me.

Behind all my mother's negative comments was her urge to keep me safe. I remembered the night I woke in feverish delirium. It was in January 1965. The doctor had told my mother that my life was in danger from encephalitis. I had not eaten for nine days. I awoke to see my mother floating above me. In reality, she had slept on the floor beside my bed and when she heard me stir, she thought that my fever might have broken. She had pushed herself up from the floorboards and bowed over me, floating into my field of vision. My recovery was long but my entire family supported me throughout.

I spotted a large, dark figure in the distance a few minutes later. My new driver and new adventures awaited me.

Chapter Nineteen: Bones from the River

David and I arrived punctually at Am Brink 7, an old village house in Ruehstaedt. An empty gilt picture frame hung on a wall and visible through it were multiple layers of wallpaper that proved the house's provenance back to the 1700s, a veritable peeling back of decor styles. Our vivacious hostess, Vera Wildgruber, had prepared homemade chicken soup and set out cheeses and bread. Vera was the editor of a book of stories about the Elbe River.[16] She had travelled by train from its source to its mouth. She contacted Constanze to say she would round up local period witnesses when she read about my project in the local newspaper.

Vera was the president of the local history group in Ruehstaedt, a task she'd taken over from a lady who would be at the later meeting in the nearby Rosenhof Pub. The mayor was also expected. An excited group took up most of the side section of the restaurant when we arrived. David was introduced, but left to go stork-spotting. Ruehstaedt was known as Germany's premier stork town.

There was uncertainty about how to start, but a grey-haired man named Siegfried Appel, a WWII child witness, needed to leave early. I'd not done a group interview up to this point and found the crowd of elderly, giggling ladies, daunting. I decided to focus on Siegfried; he was particularly edgy. With just a nod he was into his story. I found out later he'd written his stories into a book and that was why they came out quickly as polished narratives.[17]

---

[16] *Elbische Impressionen: Gedichte und Erzaehlungen von der Quelle der Labe bis zur Elbmuendung,* Verlag am Brink, 1997

[17] Siegfried Appel published *Prignitzer Landleben: ein heimattreuer Quitzoebler errinert sich* with Georg Gruenberg Verlag in 2010

He explained that no one had been interested in leading the German troops during chaotic times in May 1945. His family had a farm in Quitzoebel, which was down river from the pub where we were sitting. He started to describe what he saw on May 8, 1945, when he was 13. The American loudspeakers kept repeating that any German soldier not across the Elbe by noon would be a Russian PoW.

I looked at Siegfried, another child witness, and tried to see the child in the elder in front of me. I saw only a well-preserved 76-year-old in a hurry.

"I listened to the Quitzoebel bell," Siegfried said. "The American ferries stopped transporting disarmed German soldiers when it had tolled 12 times. I've not forgotten what I saw. It stays with you." Siegfried paused to wipe spittle away.

"The soldiers panicked. The strong swimmers ran fully dressed down the sand dunes into 12 degree centigrade waters hoping to make it across to the Americans. Others stripped down to underwear, grabbed benzene canisters or wooden planks and followed into the river.

"It didn't take long. The Elbe's currents seized them. I thought to myself, if I can hear their cries for help carried over the river, the soldiers remaining on land could too. It didn't matter. More soldiers rushed down the dunes. Like stampeded cattle, they kept rushing into the cold waters, wave after wave. They wouldn't stop." Siegfried shook his head with the memory of the senseless stampede. I read later that a "suicide psychosis" took root among Germans late in the war, especially in lands on which the Red Army advanced. Thanks to the anti-Russian propaganda that the Nazis whipped up, those soldiers Siegfried Appel saw, were suicidal.

"The Elbe claimed the shivering soldiers clutching parts of rafts, barrels, planks, fuel drums. The few rafts that made it whole to the river, swirled in circles. Their passengers cried out, '*Hilfe*! Help! *Hilfe*!' Who could help them?"

Siegfried let those images sink in before he explained that when the Russians came they fixed bayonets and waved automatic weapons to deter the panicked rush to the river. By this time, ship traffic and corpses made crossing the river all but impossible.

Siegfried waved his arms and shouted at us, "*Stoi! Stoi! Dawai! Dawai! Nasat! Nasat!/* Halt! Halt! Quickly! Quickly! Back! Back!"

We sat back in our seats, startled by his commands. He must have been a teacher, I thought. He knew how to get attention. He continued his story while our hearts pumped excitedly.

"The Russians chased me away at this point. I took field glasses I had at my house, scavenged from abandoned German equipment. I saw a bowed, bare-headed column of German soldiers, the width of a street, kicking up dust as they shuffled in the direction of Roddan. Armed escorts were taking them to slave labour in Russia."

We thought Siegfried was done, but, he waved his index finger back and forth to say, no, no, while he scanned his listeners with a slight smile. "This is the June part your Oma would have seen. Corpse duty." Siegfried began with a broad outline that it had been an unusually hot spring. He was on burial detail when they found the bloated corpses of May. They wore tattered uniforms besmeared with mud and had lodged at various points in the sedge and rushes along the river's edge. The burial detail interred these remains in local cemeteries.

"In June when your Oma came through this area, we still found corpses among the grasses and reeds. Anyone could have stumbled on them. We buried those we found. Later, when I was out with my grandfather ploughing, if we found an occasional bone or a body part eaten away by maggots, we rolled those into shallow pits. I had a spade along for that."

Still picturing those body parts, Siegfried commented, "Without marking the spot, or registering the find, we did the same thing on the next occasion we found bones from the river. These remains were MIAs, missing in action." Siegfried's last comment before he rushed away was, "Somewhere family still wait to hear."

Siegfried, had been a dynamic storyteller, but he was tightly wound, almost snappish, the way my mother was. I wondered how corpse duty at 13-years-of age had impacted his life. Child period witnesses Eva, Siegfried Tauch and Siegfried Appel had seen dead people, dismembered or burned corpses and body parts. Eva had seen two women whose legs had burned from the feet to the the knees as they lay dying. I had been listening to the testimony of period witnesses traumatized as children. Their stories added to the atmosphere of the period through which my mother and grandmother lived.

I thought then about Oma coming across body parts on her walk. Would she have been shocked or was she inured to suffering by then? In Theresienstadt the inmates worked to earn rations. Oma had worked for the Department of Social Hygiene that psychiatrist Viktor Frankl set up during his time there. The unit had started as a triage for those entering Theresienstadt who might commit suicide when they saw under what atrocious conditions they had to live. Oma's job was to help the dying find meaning in what little remained of their lives. Oma had held the hand of Death, many times.

I could not dwell on Oma for long. The group looked at me expectantly. I re-focused to ask them about those passing through the area, people Oma might have encountered.

I was told the first people fleeing to Ruehstaedt were those evacuated as a result of the bombings of Berlin and Hamburg. One teacher came from Hamburg with 14 students. A steady stream of evacuees arrived by train and bus to swell Ruehstaedt's population.

The earliest refugees arrived as a result of expulsions from lands the Russian army crossed on their push towards the Elbe. Before June 1945, the Russians drove 400,000 Germans, or those with a German heritage, over the Oder and Neisse Rivers. They gave families days, sometimes just hours, to get out of homes they had occupied for generations. Oma blended in with the expelled "ethnic" Germans.

The diminutive, white-haired Gertrud Sasse, to my right, cleared her throat. I was surprised when the group fell silent. Obviously, she was a respected storyteller. Gertrud indicated by raising her gnarled hand that she was ready. We waited, and when she held us in her thrall, she began.

"In the Rosenhof Pub, where we sit now, the farmers divided up these refugee families. They were turtles, these poor people. They carried what they had on their backs. Siegfried Appel's people took in an entire family driven out of Warthenau. The mayor back then took in 16 refugees. My family housed three refugees in the living room. When another couple arrived with four children, a horse, wagon, and cow, our family supplied them with beds and gave them the second kitchen."

Gertrud gave further details about how her family and the refugees in her house cooperated before a second wave of refugees came from Potsdam in June and July. In the fall Ruehstaedt was temporarily overrun by the Sudeten-Germans from Czechoslovakia. They had livestock and ovens on their wagons but nevertheless starved. Gertrud's mother gave what she could.

Gertrud had asked, "Why are you doing this mother?"

"I can't help it, Gertrud," she'd said, "when I see them, I have to help."

Gertrud looked at me before she continued. I felt that she had saved a part of her story about the desperate times for me. "By summertime, I realized that some female refugees were escapees from camps, or death marches, maybe even officially released concentration camp survivors, like your Oma. The Russians ordered us to give them food and clothing. We gave when asked, as much as we could. We also secretly warned them not to travel at night, because of the danger of rape." Caught mid-sentence in this fearful memory, Gertrud awakened to the Rosenhof surroundings.

Ulla Seeger, the teacher, finally found an entry point. I was not used to cramming this many interviews into one night, but I decided to go with it. The blonde, middle-aged teacher was keen to describe how her students had brought to light the history of the Sachsenhausen satellite slave labour camp, formerly situated between Quitzoebel, Gloewen and Nitzow.

Ulla's students had not been satisfied with only research. They had worked to establish a permanent memorial to the local slave labour camp for future generations to know what happened there. They sent invitations to the unveiling. The invitations included state and local dignitaries, the commanding officer of the nearby military establishment and survivors.

Gloewen camp survivors, Joseph Rotbaum-Ribo and Abram Lancman, stepped forward to join two proud young people to cut the ribbon for the memorial on September 1, 2004, as all 140 students of the Bad Wilsnack Composite School watched. Mr. Ribo and Mr. Lancman had traveled from Israel to participate in this dedication. Ulla read from a letter that one of them wrote later:

> ...as I stood next to the memorial stone in the midst of German students and teachers, I was transported back to the years when I had to break up stones and carry them on my back. I would never have dreamed that one day a stone would serve as a permanent warning. I don't know if you noticed my emotions during the ceremony, but I temporarily lost my composure for just in those seconds, during which sad memories captured me, a student handed me a bouquet. Flowers from German youth, who willingly, bravely, and in full recognition of German responsibility, engaged themselves with the most horrendous acts of the past!

As a retired teacher, I was proud that these young Germans had taken the project to such a touching ending. It showed that reconciliation and moving on were possible.

Ulla held the floor as she quickly painted a picture of the slave labourers from Sachsenhausen. The Polish men had experience with munitions from the factory at Pionski in the Radom Ghetto. The 500 Hungarian Jewesses, who arrived August 1944, had already survived Auschwitz, Kaiserwald, Riga and Stutthof, places where Oma's uncles, aunts and cousins had died.

The combined 771 men and women were mostly between the ages of 18 and 24, young people tragically seized from their lives and their futures as scientists, technicians, home makers, artists or whatever new careers the future held. They lived instead, separated by barbed wire in wooden barracks behind a guarded, electrified fence. They were cold and undernourished. Their chief work was the most dangerous part of munitions reclamation and manufacture; they also felled trees and dug ditches. When Gloewen closed in February 1945, some of the young people were sent to the ARADO airplane factory in Rathenau; others found their final destiny in Sachsenhausen and Bergen-Belsen. The SS drove the few surviving Gloewen inmates towards Ravensbruck as the Americans approached. The student research showed that some escaped into the forest.

A period witness blurted out at this point, "Our family gave food to the slave labourers working on the Havel Canal, the ones who lived in barracks in Abbendorf." The period witnesses eagerly regained focus with this assertion. Ulla Seeger didn't mind. Students from the school still tended the gardens of the memorial and the small book, *Memories of Borrowed Times (2007),* like the memorial stone, was forever.

I didn't mind the change of speakers. The actions of the young people to create the memorial showed they acknowledged the past. They were part of a new generation of remembering. I could learn from them that I didn't need to carry the sins of the past on my back like a sinister Saint Nicholas with a sack full of victims' ashes. I knew that image because my parents paid a neighbour in Hamburg to come dressed up as Saint Nicholas, to visit us on Christmas Eve. In the German tradition he carried a *Rute*/bundled sticks to punish bad children and two sacks, one which held ashes and the other gifts. My mother always said it was the *Rute* and the ashes for me. I no longer felt that was so.

I told the group at the Rosenhof Pub that I no longer believed in coincidence. I had seen the Gloewen memorial by taking the wrong path. I met the kindly "Hero of the Havel" by ending up on the wrong side of the river. And now, I had met them and heard their stories which gave me much to ponder. I was obtaining context and a great sense of what Oma was up against. There was "just-in-time" miracle work going on and I was the better for it.

David and I drove back to Wittenberge sharing the wonders of the evening. He had seen a great many sights that included lucky storks and I had a way forward. There was a beautiful soft pink glow over the river.

The voices of the Rosenhof Pub resonated with me that night. Bottled up trauma had found a "talking cure". I was overwhelmed by the generosity of these period witnesses who shared painful memories. These men and women, traumatized as children by war, had processed their experiences enough to share them. They wanted to be honest about the past.

Chapter Twenty: Men's Day Warms Up

I was sent from the lovely evening in the Rosenhof Pub with dire warnings: "Don't walk tomorrow. It's Men's Day! They will all be drunk! You won't get by them on the bicycle path!" The period witnesses, and even the mayor, clucked with concern. I risked an excess of male merriment by walking on May 1st.

Well, so be it, I said to myself, but I did take precautions. I determined to make it to my start point before the day was far along. Revelers tended to start late. I noted the places where beer wagons and tents had gone up as my driver took me to Ruehstaedt. These were bound to be hot spots of hooliganism. When the driver stopped to leave me on a quiet morning street, there by sheer coincidence stood my favourite storyteller from the previous evening, Gertrud Sasse holding firmly to a cane. She and I walked slowly towards her church; we stopped at the house in which she was born.

She clasped my hands and said, "Always look after one another. That's what my mother said." I went with Gertrud into the bright interior of her church, a few steps forward down the aisle. She pointed to the altar.

"That's where I was baptized; that's where I was married and when the time comes, my urn will stand there." Gertrud said these words with total acceptance. She had made her peace. I left the woman I imagined a helper to Oma, haloed by light from stained glass windows. The frail woman and the town of Ruehstaedt were a revelation about accepting Germany, past and present.

Church bells tolled; their clamour told me it was time to go. I had to beat those hordes of May Day men. I sidestepped a castle-hotel painted hot pink, dashed past overgrown gardens, and startled a stork. I was just about to scale the tall dyke by the Elbe, when I saw cyclists in the distance.

Oh no! They were already here, the bacchanalian boys of the bicycle path! You're in for it now, I thought. But wait. I saw women in the forefront of the ten or more riders as I looked through my zoom lens ready to capture the first May Day revelers. Three timid males took up the rear behind bold Brunhildes who rapidly pumped sturdy legs. Men's Day? Not so tough.

The cycling groups were tame couples and subdued families over the next hours. I eventually reached a grove where loud music blared from an event tent and where young serving wenches sat languidly on the grass among beer wagons. I scrutinized the desultory dryads lolling nearby as I slurped freshly brewed coffee. They were done up like extras for a Bavarian B movie, tight-fitting dirndls squeezed breasts into full view. I spotted the first males lusting for beer at this point. The pretty young women sprang to attention, delighted to be in business. The girls fiddled with a reluctant spigot and the men salivated. I headed off.

I went against the tide of larger groups whose bicycles were garnished with wilted spring wildflowers. There was an air of gaiety about those going upstream to the spawning ground of merriment. I was eager to get away from the congestion when I saw a sign in German that granted permission to walk on the old dykes. I headed quickly up a green bank to find myself under a canopy of trees on an overgrown old dyke that curved past cottages. In one yard I noted a man talking on a cell phone, obviously someone who had uttered impious prayers for a handy. I looked once, then twice. It was our hotel manager. Not so isolated after all.

The rowdier cyclists from around the next bend peppered me with sarcastic comments: "Lost your bike? What, on foot? Aren't you going the wrong way?"

I just smiled. Now and then the sinuous old dyke spat me back to the road. In one village, I ventured into the open gate of a small graveyard. Siegfried Appel had talked the previous night about placing the corpses from that hot spring of 1945 in common graves. I searched for a marker for the unknown soldiers of WWII. There it was, the marker for bones from the river.

At the next bend in the road, hundreds of bicycles stood and leaned as their owners drank at tables and benches set up in the curve of the road. No cars could get through. The revelers were younger, but families were still in view.

I saw the first group of loutish teenagers on the outskirts of the next little village. They walked with a slouch and sported comic hats which they thought granted them immunity for whatever tomfoolery crossed their minds. Their rowdy actions did not register on the parents and grandparents nearby.

It was back to the ramrod straight new dyke to face the growing throng after I savoured a strawberry torte on a terrazzo. The stewed revelers, thereafter, let go with a steady stream of wisecracks spurred on by alcohol and the bravado of group behaviour. I was routinely jostled off the path. Thank goodness I was getting closer to the many-spanned railroad bridge of Wittenberge.

I found the very spot where David and I had stopped the night before to take in the pink sunset. To my right, the clock tower of the vacant Singer Sewing Machine factory loomed from its surrounding of deserted industrial buildings. My mother had been proud of the Singer Sewing machine my father bought for her. The Wittenberge factory reminded me that she'd outfitted our first Canadian house and all of us. I admired my mother's design and sewing skills.

Further ahead, I saw that a beer-dispensing truck was getting a workout in the bend where the road curved away from the Elbe. I watched from a distance as one young man pulled away from the party with his hand to his fly. It most definitely was Men's Day.

My own representative for Men's Day waited at the hotel. David and I strolled in a lovely square where a brass band *oom pah-pahed*. We blended in among Wittenberge's more staid citizens who enjoyed the music, sunshine, sizzle of sausages and brass harmonies. The upstream frenzy of Men's Day had long since ebbed from these bodies.

There was time for just a little rest before the tour with the official town guide. Juergen Schmidt was due to meet us at Hotel Prignitz. Constanze had scheduled us to meet WWII period witnesses in the hotel's breakfast room after his tour of Wittenberge. The manager was abuzz over the publicity.

Our guide arrived punctually, clad in full Prussian regalia. He was a tall, robust man, who sweated profusely. The blue woollen cape of a Night Guard hung dashingly over his homemade uniform. He looked very like a Civil War re-enactor, but, we were about to enjoy a different historical ride.

The unprepossessing, rundown former East German town took on an interesting air in the next hour. We were stared at by passers-by as we toured, but, no wonder. We traveled in the company of a 1.8 metre tall, heavy-set gentleman sweating under a Prussian blue, woollen cape. Sometimes those who stopped to stare, listened to Juergen's historical patter.

"Wittenberge didn't have the advantage of a medieval centre. Its growth was organic around industries," Juergen began. "Being situated halfway between Hamburg and Berlin, Wittenberge's heyday arrived when the *Deutsche Bahn* made its train station into a repair depot. The town became a major transportation hub before the turn of the 20th century. Wittenberge's successful merchants demonstrated their wealth by building a variety of Jugendstil buildings."

Juergen Schmidt walked us by the showiest merchant homes. He noted variations in architecture that included the use of emerald-green accent tiles and the pre-Bauhaus use of alternating shapes and colours. One of the finest buildings combined the geometric and floral aspects of Jugendstil. Slowly the sombre cement atmosphere of DDR Wittenberge lifted. We halted before a grand, corner house where Juergen's mother Ingeborg had lived as a young girl.

"The attic gallery was so large that she rode her bicycle around it," our guide said.

Only Juergen's mother and partner waited back at Hotel Prignitz. I was not disappointed by the turnout. Fewer witnesses made interviews easier. We were about to learn more than we cared to know about Juergen and Ingeborg Schmidt.

Early on in the discussion we learned that Juergen's father, SS Squad Leader Herbert Schmidt, had been in the elite fighting corps called *Leibstandarte SS Adolf Hitler,* which translated to Hitler's Bodyguard. Later research bore out why I had felt prickles down my back when I heard that. David's interest was palpable.

Although the *Leibstandarte* had morphed from its initial purpose as protection for Adolf Hitler into a tough fighting unit of up to 25,000 men and 400 Panzers, constant throughout its metamorphoses was the fact that it was filled with fanatical National Socialists. Evidence of this fanaticism was the 1940 slaughter of more than 80 British PoWs at Wormhout in Flanders, the 1943 massacre of more than 20 Jews in the Lake Maggiore area of Italy, and the 1945 murder at Malmedy in France of 72 U.S. soldiers who had surrendered. Our Herr Schmidt, the elder, could not have evaded participation in at least one of these three incidents.

David, who usually disappeared once interviews started, was fascinated to be this close to the history of a significant SS corps. Granted, we had the wife and son, and not the SS Squad Leader before us. Nevertheless, David took over. He had prosecuted the Wasyl Odynsky Denaturalization Case in Canada's Federal Court; he knew war crimes cases and was an accomplished interrogator. I translated as he skilfully plumbed our *Leibstandarte* witnesses. Ingeborg and Juergen dodged and parried as David tried to box them in, to catch their inconsistencies. The pair was proficiently evasive. We would never know if David got close to the true SS Squad Leader Schmidt's past. We did learn about Ingeborg.

Ingeborg Schmidt was born in 1926. She had not married her *Leibstandarte,* Herbert, until 1950, when he returned after his period as a PoW in Russia. She'd waited for her "giant" to whom she was engaged in 1945 when she was 19. The tiny, vivacious blonde with a warm smile asserted that her beloved was forced into the SS because of his size. His 1.92 cm height was the "Aryan ideal" for this unit. What was a tall man to do?

Ingeborg eventually started the narrative of her own life. She told us that her parents were persecuted in 1933 when the Nazis took power because they were ardent socialists. She continued her education until she was 17, when called up to train as a bus conductor.

Ingeborg's hands fluttered by her face as she talked about the pounding of bombs, the near misses, and thunderous noise. She was clearly a nervous person and driving buses in Berlin in the 1940s contributed to that. She thought she would get a break from the interminable bombings when she went to visit her aunt in Hamburg.

"Just as my train pulled into Hamburg's *Hauptbahnhof*/main station," Ingeborg said, "the sirens sounded. My aunt was too excited to go into the cellar." Ingeborg paused and her nervous smile disappeared.

"Finally when bombs fell nearby, we dashed downstairs. My cousin rushed to his volunteer duty with the Fire Department. He was developmentally delayed, but every set of hands was welcome at that time. We didn't know it but *Operation Gomorrah* was underway. Hamburg in the last week of July 1943 was being obliterated as we sat in the shelter at *Bundes Strasse*."

"Bundes Street," I interrupted. "That's near where my Oma and mother were. Their building at Papendamm survived."

Ingeborg let that register and then continued with a slight tremor, "We weren't that lucky. A direct hit destroyed all four stories above us. We were entombed. We'd have died, but for my cousin. He led members of the fire department to the exact spot where we were buried. Imagine doing that? He refused to leave. Only when he kept digging with blood dripping from his fingers did the others help. Eventually, they heard us."

Ingeborg was lost in the moment when she was buried under a building. Then she shook herself and went on. "My aunt and I exhausted ourselves grappling upwards. Our hands were raw. When we were dug out we saw that nothing stood near where we were. We picked our way through unspeakable debris, things in it I can't mention; then I saw worse. People we passed near the Alster Lake were burning. Their heads and arms smoked. Neither water nor blankets put out the glow that came from them. The white phosphorus the Allies used to create smoke couldn't be put out." Ingeborg backed up on her chair and began again with a memory she meant to be lighter.

"At one point we saw a parrot, his cage standing askew in the ruins. The parrot repeated what he'd heard on the radio, 'The damages are limited; we are well. The damages are limited; we are well.' The macabre message sounded like a broken record as we made our way through piles of debris to find an intact train station outside Hamburg, to get back to Berlin."

Ingeborg went on to explain that when she couldn't take the bombing anymore, she took three days on foot to make it from Berlin to Wittenberge. She found out later that when Berlin was taken that her fiance was caught in the pincer between the Allies and Russians. He was sent as a prisoner to the West Ukraine, to a camp near Tula.

"Each time they let prisoners go, they first had to raise their arms," Ingeborg said. "SS had blood types tattooed in their armpits. Herbert was one of the last to go home."

Back in Wittenberge in the post-war days, Ingeborg watched the area swell with 26,000 refugees that poured in from East Prussia, Pomerania and the Sudetenland. Ethnic Germans were on the move, expelled from their homes. I'd heard that story. These were the people in the Elbe River Valley with Oma. The Sudeten-Germans had mostly loved Hitler; others in the valley were his victims.

Ingeborg knew that people who were released from concentration camps were underway, as well as the refugees. When I asked how Oma might have made it through the Wittenberge area, Juergen offered an explanation.

"The farmers back then had communal field barns dotted through the region. These collective structures were larger than normal barns; they were usually open." Both Juergen and Ingeborg concurred that these barns were used by refugees, and concentration-camp prisoners.

"Released concentration-camp prisoners weren't welcome," added Juergen. He'd heard of an instance in a place called Gardlegen where in the days of lawlessness at the end of the war Jews were driven into one of these communal barns. "It was locked and set on fire." Juergen noted that few communal barns remained. "Times have changed."

Ingeborg continued to outline her life story. On January 21, 1950, she married Herbert Schmidt and their only child, our guide, was born in 1952. By 1953, the former SS man was a manager in the Singer Sewing Machine factory which, after a turn as a producer of wartime goods, was once again making sewing machines on DDR supplied equipment. The original 1904 German equipment had been trundled off as war reparations to Podosk, Russia. Ingeborg gave up her management position in transportation to become a "worker" so that Juergen could go to one of the better DDR schools, one reserved for the children of workers.

The tag-team of mother and son at this point handed off to son. Juergen Schmidt, born seven years after the war was not a period witness for WWII. He explained how he had studied Marx, became a history teacher and devoted himself to the Russian cause as he climbed in the ranks of the Communist Party. He followed in the footsteps of his ardent socialist grandfather and a father who had been a member of a fanatical SS unit. By his own admission, Juergen described himself as a fervent communist. Then came the unification of East and West Germany. The heavy-set man hung his head in shame.

"I lost everything when the DDR was gone, even my self-respect. People spat at me in the streets of Wittenberge, resentful of my former communist fervour. I did a lot of soul searching. It took me a long time to put myself together again. In the end, I realized I didn't want to believe in any ideology." Juergen's voice trailed off. When he started again, he slowly described how he reinvented himself as the tour guide sitting before us.

Juergen Schmidt handed me a card that read Juergen Schmidt, *Hofnarr*/Court Jester. Our Prussian tour guide, as it turned out, also rented himself out as a court jester!

It was beyond irony. Constanze's press release made it clear I was following in the footsteps of my Jewish grandmother and yet the son of an SS Officer in a unit besmirched with war crimes had come forward, a man who had reinvented himself as a combination Prussian officer and court jester. How was that possible?

Weren't these two persons sitting in front of me, Ingeborg and Juergen Schmidt, as close as I would get to touching the very underpinnings of what made my Jewish family members suffer and die? It felt like it. My random meetings had seemed "fated" up to this point. They informed me about how Oma made her perilous journey in 1945, led me towards shedding my German war guilt, and provided insights about my troubled relationship with my mother. But, this encounter?

I pondered Ingeborg's testimony. She had shown no signs of guilt, no remorse. She had stood by as evil happened; then she'd married an SS man implicated in war crimes. At the same time, she'd been 13 when the war started and had experienced the worst bombings of the war. Heck, even a building had collapsed on her.

In my ambiguity towards Ingeborg and Juergen I saw that being born in Germany after May 1945 did not immediately mean that the child was "home free". Ingeborg and Juergen showed it was important to gauge the degree to which Nazi propaganda had tainted the parent and been transmitted to the child. With Ingeborg and Juergen I was looking into the heart of complicity and whether or not it could be transmitted. I was meant to learn more from the period witnesses than just what Oma had seen in June 1945.

I had sought out period witnesses with one intent and now I saw that their forthright narratives were gifted for deeper purposes. Thankfully I had more time to walk and to *worstle*/work it through. Would I come to understand why fate had set these particular period witnesses in front of me?

Chapter Twenty-One: The Parable of the Sheep

My fifteen seconds of fame arrived in Wittenberge. The hotel manager buzzed around during breakfast waving a full page spread in the local newspaper. I looked good in the gauzy photos. The manager wanted more photos to submit to a hotelier magazine that had a section for prominent people. I could not deny him. I basked in my ascendancy to "prominence".

David dropped me off on the bicycle path afterwards. It was a cool, sunny day. The Elbe was just beyond its containing dyke. Soon I heard unaccustomed sounds from the river. The sound of laughter. A rowing scull, a first on the walk, glided past. The men laughed as they rowed. They were pushing themselves but having fun, and I was too.

It was wetlands all the way until the next settlement. I loved that the frogs sang, the storks clapped, the cuckoos called, the ducks jabbered incessantly and the small speedy birds emitted distinctive trills. I startled a pair of swans and their subsequent ponderous liftoff had me root: "Come on, come on, you can make it!"

I saw my first pig when I approached Luetkenwisch. I had been underway for over a month and had spotted nary a pig. Where were the pigs that supplied the *Bockwursts, Knackwursts, Bratwursts*, and schnitzel I consumed? There was one now, roasting on an outdoor spit, for a wedding.

I snapped photos of the succulent meal-in-the-making as storm clouds gathered and the first droplets fell. I took out my umbrella, then my red raincoat. A sunny day turned threatening as I waited for the ferry crossing the Elbe. Constanze's route had me constantly shift sides of the river. My day's destination, red-brick

Schnackenburg, was on the other side, set against foreboding puffs of heavy grey clouds. The heavens released a torrential downpour just as I reached the Border Museum-Schnackenburg.

I rushed inside the museum which documented the DDR's draconian border control. A watch-tower, remnants of wire fencing, and a patrol boat equipped with huge floodlights sat in the yard. They gave an ominous feel to the place. In the half-light of the storm, I imagined desperate refugees caught in spotlights as they attempted to cross the river to freedom. The repression of the former DDR was here in this stormy, overcast place.

The sun reappeared almost as quickly as the skies had turned to rain. I had only a few moments to walk around a more cheerful Schnackenburg. I found out on the trip back to Wittenberge that the current driver's family had fled Schlesien as part of the massive Russian displacement of peoples in 1945. I realized as he spoke that former refugees were all around me. I had once read that the Germans who returned from WWII were not the same ones who had left to go to war. I finally understood. Ethnic Germans from lands to the east took the places of the war dead in West Germany's postwar mix of peoples.

The next morning the driver re-deposited me in Schnackenburg. I headed off cheerfully, even though I knew that I faced an 11.5 kilometres stretch where there was no human settlement, not even a crossroad. It would be just me and the wildlife. That day the wildlife included mosquitoes.

I slathered myself with insect repellent, but still swatted the blighters. The repellent kept them from biting, but the huge swarms made the going uncomfortable. I ran for short stretches to see if I could escape. No. My tantalizing blood drew them on. I was pleased to see the flocks of sheep that grazed by the river thinking they would provide diversionary blood for the vampire spawn. I started up the sheep dialogue I had enjoyed since Magdeburg. Ah, the rewarding *baa*s I received!

I was almost past another long sheep enclosure when I spotted a teenage lamb with its feet in the air. It jerked spasmodically with the current from the electric fence going through its body. The lamb had slipped on the muddy slope by the river and could not right itself. It was trapped against the electric fence. Its entire body had a spasm every minute or so. One lamb occasionally went over to see what was going on. The rest of the flock, halfway up the slope, looked over to the baleful, bleating lamb only now and then. Otherwise they went about their grass-chomping business. Freddy was down. Too bad.

I stood fixed to the path. I could not move, not while the lamb quivered and suffered. I looked for help. Who was I kidding? There had not been another person for 90 minutes. I pondered how to reach the lamb and wondered just how much current was in an electric fence. Obviously enough to go through a thick coat of wool. I stood transfixed, waiting, uncertain about the danger to myself. I looked both ways on the path. Nothing. Time ticked by. I could not leave.

I was planning improbable rescues in my head when I spotted a speck, a distant cyclist. I waited. The cyclist would surely stop. But, he had in earplugs and was concentrated. He did not notice the agitated person near the bicycle path. I moved to stand in his way.

After an abrupt halt, the fit, middle-aged cyclist listened to my tale and marveled. Surely I did not intend to rescue a sheep? Only when I took off my day pack, left my camera on the electrical box that fed the current into the fence and headed down the hill, did the gentleman understand that the rescue was on.

I moved quickly to stand in the oozing mud on the riverside of the enclosure, right by the lamb in spasm. I reached over the low fence and grabbed the hind legs attempting to heave the dead weight of the animal away from the electricity. I was still struggling with the weight when two hands grabbed the forelegs. The gentleman had somehow made it into the enclosure and now helped free the lamb.

The lamb lay stunned, as if dead. We both looked on. Silence. I thought it had all been futile. The lamb was overloaded with electricity. Then suddenly, the lamb sprang to life and ran bleating towards the solid line of sheep that had come over to watch the intervention. Whatever the lamb said, there was a babble of *baas* in response, a regular frolic. Freddy was alive!

I realized how the gentleman got into the enclosure when he used his thick running shoe to step down the fence. Why had I not thought of that? I had on rubber-soled shoes. Then he righted the fence, we exchanged a few pleasantries and with ear plugs reinserted, he was off. The sheep saga was over. But was it?

I told the lamb rescue story a few times thereafter and I was astounded by the responses:

"It was only a lamb, why rescue it?"one person asked.

"Wasn't the lamb the shepherd's responsibility?" another pointed out.

I was aghast. What seemed clear, don't turn your back on suffering, had qualifiers. A few people even felt I should not have importuned the cyclist. It was impolite.

What was going on? Neither Judy nor Oma, nor David would have had questions. I would have had to run after them down the hill, into the mud to assist *them* with the rescue! I knew that we weren't wrong. My Jewish friend Bev later confirmed I'd done right when she told me about *tikkun olam.*[18] The phrase referred to the responsibility to fix the tear in the universe—fixing what is wrong. I believed and acted on that to the best of my abilities; others acted, if at all, only when prompted or pushed, such as the gentleman on the bicycle.

I plodded on to Moedlich directly after that lamb incident. I was to meet a new driver there. I had a small meal on the patio of a riverside restaurant. I had made good time, despite the delay occasioned by the lamb. This particular restaurant had an eel pond at its side and eel on the menu. That was new. I remembered my father's glee as he ate smoked eel. It was a total "yuck" for me. Once again, differences in people. But, what if life and death were involved, action required, and it was not a mere matter of taste? *Tikkun olam.*

I moved to sit on a rock near the road once I was done my meal and not long after, a van that sported a trailer pulled up and a short, muscled man bounced out. I immediately took to the

[18] *Tikkun olam*: Because the world is broken, human beings must repair it by committing to social justice, political activism and ethical behaviour.

chatty, entrepreneurial new driver. We had an animated conversation on the drive to Hitzacker.

David and I settled into the new boutique hotel. We had established our routines since Tangermuende and he was happy with his travel experiences and chores. We walked over a bridge into the old town which the River Jetzl had made into an island. Hitzacker, like Tangermuende, retained ancient, timbered houses. Most were sanitized after the island was swallowed by flooding in 2002 and 2006. Pictures in windows, and marks on walls, showed where we walked was then underwater. It helped us to picture different times of stress. Two small hills overlooked Hitzacker where nobles had lived centuries before. I told David that the rich guys got the high ground.

I faced a routine walk in good weather the next morning. I no longer thought of Oma's transit through the Elbe valley. I was confident I knew the dangers and desperation she had faced on the crowded Elbe floodplains. The WWII period witnesses saw to that. Now, as I neared the last leg of the walk, I relaxed in the beautiful present.

My comfort level led to a new interest in reflections. I first had looked for the colour patterns in the scenery; now, I searched for Monet-like reflections in water. The surfaces of wetland ponds provided mirrored trees, clouds and reeds; sometimes the wind slightly rippled the watery view. I looked closely for variations in these murky wonderlands where tips of reeds or breezes disturbed the illusion of a doubled world. Mirrored nature fascinated me as much as the real thing. Then at a particular moment after I had looked down upon the reflected world, I looked up to see one cloud, only one puffy cloud in the whole vast expanse of azure. It looked staged, but there it was, one cloud over Germany.

It was time to meet more WWII witnesses when I made it back to the Hitzacker hotel. Constanze had found the director of the local museum, Klaus Lehmann, and he in turn arranged the interview candidates. The hotel's host family had set a table with fine linen and china on the back patio. It was all very chic. Frau Barbara Linke, Herr Wolfgang Schulte, and the elder Frau

Marlene Kleinhans[19], mother to the proprietor, Wilfried Kleinhans, were eager to start, especially Frau Linke, who was a chatterbug. The museum director was late but we forged ahead, backwards into the time of war. Cups clattered lightly on saucers during the storytelling.

I looked up from my last tasty morsel of torte to see a woman I recognized. Why was she familiar? I realized with a gasp it was Sylvie-lyn Reif; her husband Thomas stood partly obscured behind her. My distant cousins from my father's side of the family had arrived in Hitzacker. They were my closest relatives in Germany. They had come unannounced to surprise me. It was difficult to suppress my enthusiasm and still pay proper attention to the WWII witnesses. Luckily, Sylvie-lyn joined the excited coffee and cake convocation, and before I could say we would be off, the subdued Herr Schulte said in a whisper that he still had his story to tell.

We fell silent when Wolfgang Schulte said he was a product of the Nazis' *Lebensborn* program. I had heard the term, but had scant knowledge of this Nazi scheme to breed a master race from the loins of SS officers and fair-haired "Aryan" maidens. Later research that evening fleshed out Herr Schulte's story.

The slogan, "Give the Fuehrer the Gift of a Child!", had hit a chord in young German women as smitten with Hitler and the "Aryan hero" as young women later were with the Beatles. Handsome, uniformed men were visible in newsreels and they marched through the streets, but there was a scarcity of available men. Duty took them to far fronts and made them otherwise inaccessible. Reich Leader SS Heinrich Himmler then came along with a program to encourage "racially pure" young women to have sex with handsome men in uniform in order to beget babies for Hitler. There were incentives to sweeten this "civic duty"—as if the lure of a torrid sexual encounter was not enough for sexually charged young women. Over 8,000 young women gave Hitler the gift of a child. Small wonder in these hot-house circumstances.

---

19 Marlene Kleinhans 1923-2009

Herr Schulte described his eager search for his *Lebensborn* birth parents. "I wanted to know why I was here," said Herr Schulte clearly tormented by that question. "By 1955, I'd been adopted into the family who ran this hotel. They were very good to me. I considered them my mother and father, but I wanted to know more about my biological parents. Was there any love at all involved between my birth mother and father?"

There was a strong stigma associated with illegitimate births when Himmler first created the Registered *Lebensborn* Society on December 12, 1935 and hence "the business" conducted in the 25 German locations was kept secret; records sealed. Birth mothers surrendered their newborns to the state as per prenatal agreement. They left their private and luxurious confinement and went back to wherever. The children were housed in *Lebensborn* nurseries until they were parceled out to Nazi-trained, approved homes where they were raised as the next generation for the thousand-year Reich, seeds germinated from, and cultivated for, Nazi ideology.

Herr Schulte took up his narrative and his blue eyes seemed to darken. "I was found to be a difficult child in my first *Lebensborn* home. Whenever I misbehaved, I was thrown into a bathtub and held under ice-cold water. The more I was treated that way, the more difficult I became—bed wetting, stuttering. Finally, I was moved out of the home and into the first of five foster homes. I never stayed long, because no one wanted to deal with a difficult child. I was often the fourth child because women who had four or more children had relief from work service. In every home I fought with older children to get anything at all from food to clothes."

Herr Schulte became agitated when he recalled the abuses of his early childhood. Other *Lebensborn* children fared worse. During the war years, the Nazis sent *Lebensborn* children they considered un-Aryan in appearance to concentration camps to await murder. Those still in foster care when the war ended were mostly abandoned or left in orphanages. With the stigma of Nazi ideology stuck to them, *Lebensborn* spawn were the target of humiliation and persecution.

Not so for Wolfgang Schulte. The Hitzacker hotelier's family took him in and he completed his education in a secure setting. He went on to apprentice and work in the hospitality sector after learning the industry at his adoptive parents' hotel. He pointed to an old rattan side table nearby that was once in a hotel room Hitler occupied in Hamburg, a morbid souvenir he had brought home after a successful career as a hotel manager.

"When I was able to access my records after German reunification," Wolfgang began again, "I learned they were in Hanover. I went there. I found out my father was still alive. I was very excited. I would finally be able to ask questions about the circumstances of my birth. When I tracked down my father's current address, I raced there as soon as I could. Maybe it was not wise, but I just went and rang the doorbell." There was a long pause while Wolfgang composed himself.

"He rushed to close the door. The man who is my father pressed the door shut. I thought maybe I'd been too eager and maybe a woman who shouldn't know about me was in the background. I managed to squeeze a card with my name and address in before the door shut completely. I thought, well at least he had that now. He'd be able to contact me when he has thought further about my visit. A few weeks later, I got a letter."

Herr Schulte laughed out loud with brokenhearted sarcasm. "It was a lawyer's letter. I could expect legal consequences if I ever attempted to contact him again."

Herr Schulte, a robust, handsome man in his late sixties, was near tears. He went on to apologize that since he was an infant at the time, he did not have information to help me with the story of Oma. "But, I'm a World War II witness," he said somberly. "My very being bears witness to madness." The extreme fanaticism of the Nazi times was made flesh in this shattered man.

I knew that Herr Schulte had taken upon himself the pain of telling his story so that I'd understand the reach of Nazi ideology, propaganda and its pain into the present. In him, I saw that my mother's damage sprang not just from bombing and imprisonment but from the lasting effects of Nazi ideology and edicts. My mother felt shame for being under-educated, shame for having a baby without being married (because marriage was denied her by the *Nuremberg Laws*) and shame for being designated a *Mischling*/half-breed, an outsider in her Christian circle of friends. Her successes in Canada helped put aside this shame.

After Herr Schulte's story, we heard that there was a secret oil, benzene, and rocket fuel facility nicknamed WiFo[20], just outside Hitzacker. Effective disguise had kept the massive facility from bombing during the war; only afterwards did the Allies dynamite it. The museum director who had quietly joined us during Herr Schulte's talk added that even in ruins the site was impressive. David and I became very interested.

Sylvie-lyn, Thomas, David, and I headed to a restaurant when the witnesses finally departed. We sat on a beautiful terrace that hung over the Jetzl River. The very presence of my cousins made me realize that my walk was drawing to a close. They had made it from Hamburg in a very short time. I was happy to see them, but, also sad. I was enjoying my time out of time. I did not want it to end.

David and I headed to the Toll House Museum bright and early the next morning. Herr Lehmann, the director, wanted to tour us through all four floors. What a tour it was! We picked up a smattering of everything from the book-loving duke who liked to burn witches, the history of kills made by the DDR border patrol, to the visits Queen Beatrice of the Netherlands made to Hitzacker. The queen came to attend the funerals of her in-laws, the Armbergs. I sat in the chair where Queen Beatrice signed the guest book and signed it myself. I lamented that I had forgotten my camera to record this event and Herr Lehmann commented, "At least you have your prince with you!"

I did.

David and I later went off with my cousins on a walk along the dyke at Damnatz and then, just because it was there, we headed into the local graveyard. I stopped at random by the grave

---

[20] WiFo stood for WIrtschaftliche FOrschungsgesellschaft MBH, a deceptive name even in German as it translated to Research Association for Commerce and showed no connection to a fuel storage facility

of someone called Charlotte Voigt. I noticed from the dates on her stone that she'd been cut down in her youth during WWII. David had tried the previous day to get the period witnesses to sort out who had fled where at the end of the war, but since everyone was trying to flee, and no one really knew where was safe, it was an insoluble puzzle. Charlotte Voigt, whoever she was, had lost her life in that confusion. Oma had not.

We headed back to climb the hill in Hitzacker. We were told the Jewish graves were at the summit and we were going to investigate. We climbed and found the graves hidden in a forgotten leafy grove. Vandals had scratched out the names on the German side of the stones, obviously decades before as the scratches had weathered. Hebrew letters remained untouched on the other side of the grey stones. Sylvie-lyn was incensed by the defacement. She decided to find out more about the vandals. She asked about it when we passed a lone, elderly woman tending the graves of her husband and two daughters.

"No idea," stated the woman looking up from where she knelt. "There haven't been Jews in this area for hundreds of years."

"Do you know the stones are defaced?" Sylvie-lyn asked. She directed her gaze upwards to the grove.

"Maybe *Kristallnacht,*" the lady offered. "There were hooligans that night."

"Even with no Jews in Hitzacker?" Sylvie-lyn asked.

"Let me show you something else," the lady said. She put down her hand shovel, lifted up her stiff body and picked up a cane which she wielded like a marching band director. She breezed past neat rows of war dead to the post-mortem real estate of the titled ones. She pointed with the cane and listed off names without having to pause to read them.

"Prince von... Duke of... Baron..."

Thomas knew the significance of the titles and explained them to David as we went along. So many echelons to humanity! The Armsberg graves, as all those of the nobility, were extremely well tended. I looked up towards the untended, defaced Jewish graves. At least, they had the higher ground.

We had two phone calls during breakfast the next day to indicate that Herr Lehmann had found someone for a WiFo *Tanklager* tour. We were going to see a relic of Nazi history. Our guide led the cavalcade of cars a few kilometres up the road and then we hiked a narrow dirt path. Sunlight filtered through the dense canopy as we made our way deep into the forest. The guide missed the unobtrusive WiFo entrance. He was engaged in talk with Thomas, but that was not why. No one would have found the place without specific directions and acute attention. The gate and fence enclosure, topped with barbed wire, were almost totally obscured by foliage that grew over them like a keloid scar.

The guide said as he narrated from notes, "The Nazis bought the land for the oil, benzene and rocket fuel bunkers in 1934, fenced the place in 1936, constructed the bunkers and covered the site, all before the war."

"Who could say the Nazis weren't planning war right from the beginning?" I asked rhetorically as I scanned the massive cement ruins of fuel bunkers the size of several hockey arenas.

"These trees were planted over the underground facility in 1937-38 to camouflage it," our guide narrated.

"Well, it's still working," said David as he pointed to the trees and vines that reclaimed the ruins.

"Herr Schulte said yesterday that the roads to the facility were painted green to prevent aerial reconnaissance. From the air, the complex must have looked like just another stand of trees," Sylvie-lyn said.

"No wonder the Allies couldn't find it," I said.

"They bombed the rail lines, but never hit any bunker or tunnel," our guide said.

I climbed down into one of the massive underground tunnels that brought the fuels to and from the tankers at the harbour on the Elbe River. The tunnel was the size and shape of those long barrel vaults that lead into the Coliseum in Rome. WiFo was a massive undertaking.

The guide shouted down into the hole, "The same kind of tunnel you're standing in is still in use in a Bremen fuel storage facility that the Allies didn't dynamite after the war."

"The Nazis built to last," I said and my words echoed from the depths into the trees.

"Herr Director wants to hold an open air concert in the ruins," the guide added proudly.

"Fantastic site for it." said David. He tried to capture the immensity of the place with a broad sweep of his arm.

"Resonant of more than music." Sylvie-lyn said. She tut-tutted all the while she stared around.

We tromped back and said goodbye to our guide at the cars.

From the depths of the earth, surrounded by concrete, we drove further along the highway to a rickety wooden observation tower. We climbed to the heights over the Elbe where we had a spectacular view of the green countryside: magnificent hills, dales, woods, and farmlands. Not a hint of a hidden Nazi fuel facility. A magician had waved a wand. Poof! That one cloud over Germany had disappeared.

But, the war's after-effects couldn't disappear. War's children kept it alive. I turned my mind slowly towards a new idea, a better place to be. Oma, my mother, child period witnesses, Holocaust survivors and war veterans had shown strength and resilience to forge on with their lives. I needed to champion that.

Chapter Twenty-Two: The Gypsy's Violin

All was well. Our balcony rooms at the Landhaus on the Elbe in Bleckede overlooked gardens in bloom and a charming array of church steeples. The internet hummed and we expected another set of period witnesses that evening. There was also a radio reporter on the way.

I once again had serious blisters. The bad ones I had at Meissen had never healed properly. They could not heal, not with the amount of walking I was doing. I had no difficulties finding additional blister pads in Bleckede as there were three pharmacies in the small village. They served the elderly who lingered in small shops and sidewalk cafes. The obvious lack of young people was acutely visible in the former DDR. Back at the Landhaus the radio reporter and I sat on a bench in the sunshine. She was eager to add her own imprint to the story of a time-traveller on the Elbe. Our host, Herr Dieter Kunze, drew nearer in ever decreasing semi-circles as he took photos.

That evening we were surprised by a wonderful spread of delicacies that Herr Kunze generously provided. The guests included two local reporters, Frau Ilse Meyer who had lived in nearby Alt Garg during WWII and Frau Meyer's grandson, a history buff who specialized in that fuel tank facility called WiFo. David stayed as my translation capacity was very good with all the practice I'd had. Our host drifted in and out, with a permafrost smile. He was very happy to see this event in his establishment.

The jumble of voices and impressions in the Landhaus proved even more difficult than in the Ruehstaedt pub. The sparkling-eyed Ilse Meyer stood out in the hubbub of voices. Her indomitable life force surpassed everyone's, even her grandson's. She flirted with David as if 18, not 80. David smiled at the sparks she sent his way. Like period witness Helga Gaebler upriver in Riesa, Ilse was unashamed about her involvement with the *Bund Deutscher Maedel*/ League of German Girls, a youth organization that took young girls on hikes, had them play sports and sing songs. The BDM was mandatory after all.

Not for my *Mischling*/half-breed mother, I thought as Ilse continued. My mother had to stand in the school hall while the girls in the classroom sang their "Aryan" songs and did their *Heil Hitlers!* The BDM gals, like Ilse, clearly disassociated themselves from their part in the Nazi propaganda machinery.

Ilse told us that in August 1944, when she was 17, things changed for her. She had not been seriously touched by war until then. She had barely noticed when the Hamburg Electrical Works built barracks on the Dorfstrasse near Bleckede. Those barracks housed 1,500 Croatian, Serb and Slovakian forced labourers. During my research, I continued to be astounded at the numbers of forced labourers the Reich plucked from the countries they invaded. The men in Bleckede toiled to erect what was one of Germany's most productive power plants. Ilse did notice the erection of the barracks of Camp B in her own neighbourhood on her side of the Elbe.

In the summer of 1944, ten wagons brought 500 men from Sachsenhausen Concentration Camp to Alt Garg, most of them former members of the Polish resistance. The men built three wooden barracks for themselves before they began heavy digging for the power plant. The electricity facility had been located downriver to be safe from the bombing of Hamburg that had continued after *Operation Gomorrah* and went right to the end of the war. Robbie Lavack had told me that RAF pilots like himself, had been instructed to drop leftover bombs on Hamburg. Meanwhile, barges heaped with coal daily traveled the river to keep the new power plant fired up for Hamburg.

Ilse passed *Lager B* every day as she was the one in her family designated to pick up the mail in the village. She heard men scream as the guards whipped them and once saw a prisoner hit across the face. She noted emaciated corpses piled outside the fence. These were daily loaded on trucks. The shrunken corpses were in stark contrast to the guards who Ilse described as, "obese from over-eating".

Ilse decided she wanted to answer the whispered pleas she heard from behind the barbed wire: "Potatoes, please!" She knew local farmers had potatoes.

"I was pert at 17-years; I knew how to flirt. I flashed my eyes and strutted (at which point the animated Ilse smiled girlishly at David) and when I did, my friends who were with me threw potatoes through the fence. The fat guards never caught on."

The Alt Garg prisoners were worked to breaking and died despite the young women's efforts. In October 1944, the Nazis sent 100 spent labourers to Neuengamme Concentration Camp; they replaced them with Danish and Norwegian slave workers. Replacements were again needed in December and January. Forty-nine men were buried in the cemetery at nearby Barskamp. Alt Garg was liquidated as the Allies advanced in February 1945. The remaining prisoners were sent to Hanover-Misburg, another of Neuengamme's 80 satellite camps. They went part of the way by ship along the Elbe River, that hard-working Elbe River.

Another of Ilse's stories dealt with Roma neighbours who lived in a caravan wagon near her family home. She and the Roma children went to the same small country school. Ilse cleared her throat as she readied herself for a different narrative.

"My father knew that they would come to take away the gypsies," Ilse said. "Then shortly afterwards, they'd take their goods. I went with him to look for items the family might value when they returned, things officials wouldn't suspect were missing. We decided on a violin and a few small paintings and we hid them in our attic."

"Quite some time after the war," Ilse continued, "there was a knock on our door. I didn't recognize the worn-down woman, my former schoolmate. She showed me the number tattooed on her arm and told me all her relatives were gone, murdered, including her younger sister, my classmate. As she was about to leave, I remembered the things in the attic. Tears welled up and flowed down the woman's lined face when I brought in the violin and the paintings. She handled the violin with tenderness, cradled it like an infant. It was not much, but I felt we'd done something."

It was something for Ilse to save precious items for her Roma neighbours. It was a tangible act. Just as throwing potatoes over the fence to slave labourers was an act of mercy. Could I condemn Ilse Meyer for not doing more when others had done nothing?

Ilse had further stories about her family's week long flight into the countryside to hide from the Russians, about the river corpses they buried and countless refugees who passed through their area. When I asked about someone like Oma, Ilse said, "Our hayloft was always open, and what food we had, mother shared."

Ilse told us she married quite a few years after the war. Her husband was one of the German soldiers marched to slave labour in Russia. He had three nervous breakdowns before he died. The Alt Garg Power Plant built by slave labour proved longer lasting. Ilse, who sparkled when she told her stories, fell into a sad silence at the thought of her deceased husband.

I thought of my father's words: *Immer worsteln lassen* and I realized that I had to work through the duality I felt about these period witnesses. They yielded wonderful details for the story of Oma's walk home in 1945, but, there was complexity in being a living witness to the Nazi era. Their spectrum of involvement ran from Wolfgang Schulte, the embryo fertilized by Nazi ideology, through Helga, Ilse and Ingrid the BDM girls, to Eleonore, two Siegfrieds, Eva and Ingeborg, child and teenage witnesses to bombings and death marches. They had entered the confessional of our meetings to talk; I listened.

These were the children, youth and young adults of the Hitler era, as my mother was. They had all seen too much. I was grateful they had done their part for Oma's story and for me, by showing parallels to my mother. I decided that they had been put in my way for me to learn from them and to present the nuances of complicity they represented. I would not judge them; the readers of this book could.

The spirit of storytelling lingered after the guests left. Our host Herr Kunze shared his story about the difficulties of growing up in the DDR. Once again, David and I recognized the drive it took to succeed in the former East Germany, a country devastated by the Russian occupation. Finally we said good night, after the third telephone call Dieter Kunze had from his wife on the other side of the building.

The next morning, the driver took me on our last journey together. It was a short ride to the drop-off point but I heard how he and his three sisters were driven out of Schlesien at the end of World War II, part of the flood of refugees Oma saw. The refugees were still all around me.

The driver told me to take the DDR side of the river, a path with fewer hills. I didn't need persuasion. The ferry deposited me near a former DDR checkpoint with a white tower. That day I encountered remnants of several foreboding white towers topped with dark glass. They all sported museum-type signage. I learned from them that Elbe ferries restarted in 1989, and about the numerous deaths of would-be escapees from East Germany. I purposefully ignored construction fences and went to look through the metal mesh that had once shrouded the view of freedom on the far shore. The sunny, green landscape on the west side of the Elbe was out of reach when seen through this psychic barrier.

I read display signs about the changes to the Elbe biosphere as I walked along. The security-mad DDR had cleared trees, bushes, even villages, to create a kill zone. Robert Louis Stephenson's lines, "East is east and west is west and never the twain shall meet..." ran through my mind. Even nature was sacrificed to keep East and West Germans apart.

The path kept to natural river settings until detour signs at Stiepelsen. I heard construction vehicles and knew I could not get by when I got close enough to see that the work abutted the river. Damn! I did not want to go one extra step.

Then I paused. This detour was a minor inconvenience. My five weeks along the Elbe had been a sweet romp, even with rain and blisters. My hurdles were about understanding. In 2008 I wrestled with identity, complicity, guilt and trauma. In 1945, those on death marches, harried refugees, emaciated PoWs, desperate slave labourers and Oma looked up to the same sun, saw the same river and heard cuckoos, but their walks started in the darkness of evil and continued in fear. They detoured around men with guns, corpses in the woods, body parts in the river. I had to limp around a construction site and suss out the meaning of my walk. Not quite the same.

Before long the detour led me back to a newly paved path shining brightly into the distance. I pondered as I moved painfully onward that the variegated bird song, the buzz of bees, swoop of swallows, and the swirling circles of storks overhead must have lifted the spirits of people like Oma, just a bit. They had been cut off for such a long time from things natural. Summer in the Elbe Valley was "a balm in Gilead"—just as promised in the *Bible*.

I rounded the corner to yet another wetland and stopped in awe. I heard a choral symphony. Like uncountable stars in the skies, there were thousands of frog voices, so many in fact, that my presence meant nothing. Their stunning variety in tempos and tones was incredible. The singing went far beyond the frogs and me. It was an ordained story of survival. The polliwogs I held cupped in my hands as a child in Canada were singing still. Even as I tried to capture the sound on my camera, I knew I would fail. I could not freeze in a short audio clip the eternal throbbing power of nature that the frogs represented. Just as no one can capture in words the immensity of the loss of millions of individual human beings.

I almost missed the shadow falling on me, lost in these thoughts. I slowed. A green-clad elderly gent with a leather notebook-pouch slung on his back asked, "Do you want to learn more about the biosphere?"

"Why not?"I answered.

The man hopped off his bicycle and accompanied me for some very informative kilometres. He loved to teach; I loved to learn. I heard about ice ages, the impact of the Flemish settlers on the Elbe, and the intrusions of the DDR. It was a jam-packed while before the biosphere ranger biked off to fulfill other official duties. The kindly senior with erect, military posture sped off and I wondered. What were you doing during the war? I couldn't help myself. Was it my mother's mistrust inside me? I'd need to work on that!

A little while later, I saw a brown chicken fly towards its fellows. The chickens were loose in a scenic barnyard. I had seen many a chicken in my day, but never ones prepared to fly. On the walk around Lake Ontario in 2003 I'd seen a huge chicken-raising operation where the poor roasters never got out of small constraining boxes in their entire chicken lives. Who knew that if you gave chickens room they'd fly a short distance? Imposed constraints. What did they make of us?

I saw Bleckede's prominent riverside silo ahead signalling the day's end to the walking. The Elbe continued to work beside me with passenger ships and barges going both ways. It worked now, as during WWII and other wars, without taking sides: old man river!

That night David and I were the sole guests in the Landhaus Restaurant which was closed to the public. Dieter Kunze lovingly prepared sausages from Thuringia for us. They were special sausages made with pride from a heritage family recipe. We enjoyed the tribute.

A reporter showed up after our last breakfast at the Landhaus, keenly interested in the developments of the last few days and in the testimony of the WWII witnesses the night before. She wanted to give voice to what might still be told about the past, but as a young person. We took photos on the bike path. Dieter Kunze put his arm around me in yet another uncharacteristic break in German decorum. What was going on, I thought with a smile. We had not moved from *Sie* to *Du,* the change from formal to informal speech that happened only with mutual permission. I was experiencing a warmer, more open Germany. I loved it!

Genial Herr Kunze was concerned about my blisters. He had noticed my hobble. He instructed the new driver to start six kilometres down the Elbe. The day promised to be long even with a part cut off. To add to the pressure, a reporter awaited me at 2PM in Lauenburg. There would be no leisurely pace for my poor feet.

The gentle river landscape I traversed was the usual flatland but I became nostalgic about every step because my 600 kilometres walk was drawing to a close. I was caught up by a sense of loss. I would miss the carefree days along the storied Elbe.

My major responsibility for five weeks had been to walk and talk. I was a lily of the field as I felt my way forward through nature and backwards in time. My good fortune was soon to end. I would head back to Canada to wash kitchen floors, buy groceries, cook meals, and maintain relationships. Could I keep Oma from being folded under laundry? Could I make her story and that of my Jewish ancestors matter? Could I finally forgive my mother?

The well-beloved frog song that greeted me around the next bend of the river intensified my melancholy. Then the impossible happened. Frogs appeared. For weeks I had looked for actual frogs, but I had seen only rings in the water. Now the whole pond before me bounced with life and revealed a blue-green maelstrom of amphibian heads and legs. The world was alive with frogs. I relished this sight, when through the reeds in the distance ahead I saw a swan sitting on a low-lying, wide, twig nest. It couldn't get better than this!

I read travel authors who sang the praises of rail and vehicular travel over the distancing effects of air journeys. They saw more than those poor sods. Now, but for those authors who sat navel-gazing on Walden Pond or at Tinker Creek, I had bettered them all, just by walking. Mother Nature had risen from the Elbe to walk along the bicycle path. She had bared herself for me, with frogs and swans. It was glorious. I took in a deep breath to inhale it all into my being—this beauty.

Then, conscious of my blisters, I trod gingerly on. It was painful going, but I was diverted when I reached an extended suburban stretch dotted with lovely, old, thatched-roof and beamed farmhouses. I thought of them as "talking houses" because they were adorned with old sayings in ornate German script. They talked to me of the work ethic. Not too long after, in a large yard, I saw a young foal run circles around his mother, then settle in to suckle. Both his boisterous freshness and his dependency touched me. These moments were blessings writ as large as the Elbe meanders. One had only to be open to magic to see it.

I saw Lauenburg before long and its prominent railroad bridge. I checked my watch and realized I would be 15 minutes late for the reporter. She phoned as I rounded into the harbour. She said she'd walk towards me. I would have had a greater appreciation for the old timbered, medieval buildings with guild insignia hanging over long, narrow, cobbled streets if I'd not been in such a hurry. Here was the sign for the master apothecary; there the tailor, locksmith and shoemaker plied their trades. They would all have been assisted by journeymen and apprentices, a regular hive of medieval activity. Lauenburg was as pretty as Tangermuende and Hitzacker; each had its own old-world charm.

The reporter and I headed to an open-air terrace when we met up. The famous bronze figure of a sailor who shouted across the wide Elbe graced our view over the river. Sunburned, tired, and in pain from the blisters, I engaged in yet another discussion about the journey, Oma and the beauties of Germany. The reporter pressed for more.

I still wasn't entirely sure what "more" there was. I'd gone looking for my Jewish ancestors and my grandmother's path through post-WWII Germany, but in the past weeks I'd looked into dark niches in Nazi Germany's history. I had questioned the guilt of those alive during WWII. I had been overwhelmed by the beauty of nature, the kindness of strangers, the generosity of drivers and hoteliers and the openness of the period witnesses. I had awakened childhood memories of pastries, gardens, music, sausages, and laughter. I had experienced a Germany I loved as a child, had doubted, but could love again.

It was confusing. I still had to work it out fully, but I knew two things already. I had walked my way into my Jewish heritage and past personal ownership of Germany's WWII atrocities. I was not a Nazi child. Reconciliation with my mother, that still had to come.

I found the Lauenburg hotel where David waited. We had rooms with stunning views both up and down the Elbe. We talked about the short remainder of the journey. I agreed with regret and tears that the walking had to end. I had a blister on my left foot that protruded two centimetres from the back of my heel. It is was one of several blisters on blisters.

David promised to drive to Hamburg via Lueneburg to soften the blow of abandoning the last part of my walk to Geesthacht, the target Constanze had planned. I had learned to love walking on the Lueneburger *Heide*/Heather when I was a child and this stop would be a treat. In Hamburg, we would meet up again with cousins Sylvie-lyn and Thomas. Renate and Ludwig would come from Bonn with friends Paul and Gerlinde Schwartz from Speyer with whom I had visited. My cousin Jorge, eldest of the Skrainkas, would fly in from Spain. We would celebrate my Hamburg homecoming and Oma's. I contemplated the immense difference between the two—one in 1945 and the other in 2008.

I was going to Hamburg via the beautiful Lueneburger Heide. Oma had walked the last part of a death-defying journey through ruins. With each step through the rubble of Hamburg she would have become more doubtful that her daughter was alive. At the corner of Bundes Street and Papendamm she would have seen only one building standing. It was her building, number 23. She had rushed up the stairs, out of breath, heart pounding and beat furiously on the door of the apartment. Would anyone answer?

My mother had opened and Oma fell into her arms—only to be pushed away. Why? Oma looked at what took shape. My mother cradled an infant. It was my brother, born April 24, 1945. Oma had almost crushed him. My mother, released from Fuhlsbuettel Concentration Camp in November 1944, had hidden her illegal pregnancy for another five months. She had no news about her mother and there was no news from my father who was a disarmed enemy combatant shuffled among holding pens and prisons, mostly in France. One neighbour and one aunt kept my mother supplied with whatever meagre rations they could manage.

During one of the final bombings of Hamburg, my mother, in labour at the time, had made her own way to the midwife hospital. Josef and Rosa Skrainka, who would both have been in their 60s at that time, could have helped their granddaughter and welcomed their great-grandson—but for the Holocaust.

My upcoming homecoming to Hamburg would be less dramatic and was still a few days away. David and I explored the various quaint laneways leading uphill from the ancient town of Lauenburg. We had all our meals in restaurants that overlooked the Elbe. The last evening of the official walk, we sat on the deck of our suite, as a rose-coloured sunset bathed the boats on the ever-widening silvery Elbe. The river bore flecks of light silently, onward to the sea. It would not be my last view of the Elbe, but it was one that stayed with me.

Judy and I had accomplished a great deal but David and I got further. We had met period witnesses together and had unpacked not just what they said, but the fact that they spoke at all. The talks had opened the way towards understanding different responses to trauma. The next step was that I had to place my mother's treatment of me, within the framework of her experiences, her trauma. She had been harassed, persecuted, denied education and marriage due to the *Nuremberg Laws*; she'd lost her grandparents to murder, crouched in fear during the fire-bombing of Hamburg and she'd been imprisoned. I had gone a long distance out of the way to learn about my heritage and past. I hoped that I was moving towards the correct ending with my mother.

Chapter Twenty-Three: How Did I Get Here?

I chased dreams of childhood as we made our way towards Hamburg via the Lueneburger *Heide*. I wanted to go to the source of my passion for walking, a place in memory where the air was always fresh, the sunshine warm on my skin and my family in holiday harmony.

It took considerable twists and turns before David found a small village to fit my remembrances. The heather was not in bloom, but I extrapolated from the few dried blooms left. In my mind's eye, I created fantastic fields of lavender that flowed as far as the eye could see. David and I walked on narrow paths, through fresh-smelling firs and found our way to a sunny patio.

I marveled at David's patience. He had placed the GPS god temporarily on hold and for that I was appreciative. The reservation at my favourite Hamburg hotel called out to him eventually. He insisted we get to Baseler Hof to figure out how to park the car while I partook of yet another whipped-cream topped confection.

I had stayed at the Baseler Hof with my mother in 1994 as part of a delegation of those persecuted by the Nazis, and again in 1999 on what was her final trip. My mother had wanted to say goodbye to schoolmates when her cancer was declared terminal. I had a startling insight on one of the school girl visits. We sat in Ingrid Zornig's well-appointed living room chatting over tea when she suddenly remembered her photo album and went to find it.

Ingrid and my mother had gone to the Emilie Wuestenfeld private school in Hamburg during the Nazi era. Entrance to that school was her father's last hard-wrung victory before he died of cancer five days before the start of WWII. Alfred Schilling, a Lutheran business man, expended his last efforts to ensure that his

Mischling daughter would be able to finish high school, despite the *Nuremberg Laws* which prohibited academic education past the age of 14 to anyone Jewish or part-Jewish. Only trade schools were available to *Mischlinge*/mixed breed persons. I knew that my mother was hurt that she could not go on to university.

Ingrid returned with her album and plopped her substantial bulk beside me. She leafed through the pages with quick explanations about her BDM uniform and how she had stood beside my mother. She meant that even though my mother bore the *Mischling*/half-breed stigma, she, Ingrid, had held true to her friend. She flipped the page and was suddenly giddy over a photo.

"See how close I got to Hitler," Ingrid said excitedly. "See!" Ingrid's pudgy forefinger pointed out three girls near Hitler's motor cavalcade. "That's me," she said and looked up. My mother beamed at Ingrid. She wasn't horrified at the Hitler comment. She saw only the friend who had stood by her.

And then, I got it. I finally got it. I understood my mother's insistence that she was NOT Jewish. I'd dealt with teenagers for 33 years in my career as an educator. I should have seen it. My mother was ten when the Nazis took power. Her schooling was tainted with Nazi indoctrination. She'd absorbed the same propaganda the other girls in the BDM did, about "the Jews".

When she turned into a sensitive teenager, the *Nuremberg Laws* defined her, the blonde, blue-eyed Lutheran poster-girl, as a *Mischling*/half-breed. She was declared part of this group, "the Jews", that they'd been taught to revile. She was cast out by law and cast out of her peer group at a time she wanted to belong, and for being something with which she didn't identify. It was too much for an insecure teenager whose father had just died. My mother loved her Jewish grandparents whom she visited in Vienna during the summers, but, in Hamburg among her teenage peers, she was NOT JEWISH, The declaration she'd made to me that she was not Jewish finally made sense.

But, just because my mother rejected her Jewish roots, I did not have to. In fact, I grew incrementally more proud of these roots with each step I took. Even the murdering Skrainka from 1774 didn't bother me. Abraham Skrainka had confessed, made amends and paid for his crime. All the Skrainkas I'd found since then were, and are, creative, productive, well-educated people, persons to admire. That was "my gang".

Baseler Hof, where David and I now headed in 2008, was in an area charged with memory from childhood and from the later trips with my mother. I looked forward to showing David my city. We would not have much free time before the others arrived. I had no idea what we would do with my mother's cousin, Jorge Skrainka, our friends Renate and Ludwig Hendricks, their friends and my father's relatives, Sylvie-lyn and Thomas Reif. I knew there would be at least one large supper together.

I insisted that David and I visit the Ratsweinkeller Restaurant where my father (trained as an accountant) had worked as a wine buyer to restore the restaurant's superb wine-cellar destroyed by bombing. Sitting at the bar with David was surreal. The little girl, now a grandmother, had chased her own grandmother back through time and had found parts of her within herself. I had my Oma's tenacity, her facility with languages, and her friendly way with strangers. I looked beyond the bar into the low, grey, Gothic arches of the large basement room. No curtsying little girl in the shadows. The bar mirror reflected a mature, capable woman, who sported a sunburn and sipped brandy. I also saw in that woman's eyes that the trip was not quite done.

I struggled again to sort out the meaning of the whole journey. I had started to think it through with the first reporter back in Pirna. I had refined the journey's purpose through interviews. I had parsed experiences with Judy, and played endless monologues in my head while I walked solo, but I knew there was more to the walk than figuring out how Oma made her way home in 1945 to find my mother amazingly alive in Hamburg; more even than finding the Skrainka's Jewish history and getting rid of German war guilt.

But, for now, it was time to meet the eldest of the Skrainkas, Jorge, the son of Oma's brother Robert. The Robert Skrainka family had ended up in Venezuela as a result of the pre-WWII flight from Hitler's Thousand-Year-Reich. Jorge had arrived from Spain where he now lived. I had met my mother's Spanish-speaking cousin once, a few decades before. From a flurry of emails I knew that he was determined to participate in what he considered a significant commemoration of family heritage. I was honoured.

David, Jorge, and I headed to the Baltic Sea for a getting-to-know-you outing before the others arrived. I had a flash of déjà vu when I saw a street sign "Papendamm" as we headed out of the city. I had spent the first seven years of my life living at Papendamm 23. David made the abrupt turn into the tree-lined street when I called out. We looked but I couldn't see number 23. I asked about it when a gentleman left the house where we parked.

"Oh, that's down there," he said. "I'll take you."

Sure enough, 23 Papendamm was further down the road. It was freshly painted white and much taller than I recalled, quite a splendid building really. I wanted to see the back as I remembered looking out the kitchen window into a courtyard. Without so much as minute's pause, our guide opened a gate and walked past a sunbathing lady.

"She's from Canada," he said in German, "Come to look at the place she lived." I think the sunbather was topless, but no one paid any mind. I went back to the car to get my camera to take photos of the courtyard. A lady leaned out a second storey front window and asked, "Are you the lady from Canada?"

News traveled fast. I explained a little about my history to the lady in the window and she came down to the street. We rang the bell to the flat of the eldest lady in the apartments who lived at number 25. This Frau Gertrud Haass, who was not home, had lived near us when my family immigrated to Canada. I left my card and asked the friendly lady to tell Frau Haass about me. Then, after a spate of photos, we headed to the sea.

Jorge's English was good and his calm nature suited David. We had a relaxing time as we dipped our feet into the same waters where the siblings Anna and Robert Skrainka, my Oma and Jorge's father, holidayed as young people, and where Anna's children, my mother and her brother Gottfried played with pails in the sand.

I was to meet a reporter at Papendamm the next day. Diana Zinkler was going to interview me there and then we were to head to the Elbe River for a photo session. The telephone light blinked back at Baseler Hof. There was an excited message from Frau Haass. I heard the emotion in her recorded telephone message. She remembered me, my brother, parents and Oma, in detail!

I finally spoke with Frau Haass after the usual wrong numbers, unlisted numbers and missed connections. Her strong voice trembled with emotion as she remembered the very day we left for Canada in 1954.

Diana Zinkler and the photographer waited the next day in front of 23 Papendamm. Ms Zinkler queried me for "the hook" for her story. What was there to interest a modern audience in a lady from Canada walking 600 kilometres along the Elbe River? Germans had read a great number of Holocaust stories. Was I another one?

Even then as we took photos on the steps of my former home, I did not have the full answer. I told Diana I had to excuse myself to go upstairs to meet with Frau Haass, a former neighbour.

"Could I go with you?" Diana asked eagerly when she realized I'd not seen Frau Haass for over 50 years. I saw from the sparkle in her eyes Diana thought she had found her story.

Gertrud Haass' apartment was a mirror image of my family's. As I entered what could have been my own home, Frau Haass said, "My little Angelika, I recognized you right away." We held each other in a tight embrace.

Since I was no longer seven-years-old, I pulled away a little to say, "I am already a grandmother."

To which Frau Haass answered, "Let me be your Oma."

Frau Haass folded me into her plush bosom which pillowed and comforted me. I had indeed found Oma again, now in Frau Haass' embrace. Oma's soft hand touched my face in this room of my childhood. Then the new Oma took a step back.

"What ever happened to your brother?" she asked. "He was such a little professor."

I laughed because my brother was a professor, at the University of Alberta.

Gertrud Haass remembered my mother's seamstress skills. "You were always dressed like a little doll," she said.

She remembered my well-read and well-spoken Oma. "I used to run into her when she later lived on Durchschnitt."

How was it possible that after 54 years I had found an 87-year-old lady who remembered me and my family in detail? We moved to sit on her couch and held hands. We exchanged more stories. I looked over to see if Diana Zinkler was impatient to leave. She was not. She had tears in her eyes. We were lost in the magical day created out of the sheerest happenstance. How many stars had to line up for this convergence?

When Frau Haass and I pulled apart from another long embrace that day, it was difficult for me to discern the borders to our separation. We had merged in our long, tearful embraces. Where did she end and I begin? We were all kinds of Omas mixed together. We were past and present made whole by our encounter. Walking with my Oma had done that.

After a tearful, "See you later", as David and I planned to return after the photo shoot, we headed to the Elbe, the river that had guided me to the homecoming with a new Oma. Diana and I drove through hectic Hamburg traffic with the news photographer and David following in separate cars, until we all made it to a place where the Elbe had a sandy beach-like shore.

I had never once dipped my feet into the Elbe River during 600 kilometres; now I walked into the lapping waves with shoes on. I was finally in the great river that had flowed before me from Theresienstadt for 40 days. The river paused ever so slightly to wash over my shoes before it pulled back into the currents that would take it to the ocean. The waters were soft and kind.

David and I returned to Frau Haass. By the time we arrived, she had contacted her daughter Waltraut, the little girl with whom I had played years before. That little girl was on the line from England. We remembered incidents from our childhood as we both choked back tears. Waltraut Haass-Taylor had wanted to immigrate to Canada when she was a teenager because our family's departure had impacted her greatly.

David and I sat for a while longer with Frau Haass. He enjoyed being in her elegant apartment where he glimpsed my German childhood. It was finally time to say good-bye to Frau

Haass that fateful day. The Hendricks and Schwartzes awaited us. Their hotel was close to ours, just beyond *Planten un Blomen*, the beautiful botanical garden where I'd played as a child, the garden that had supplied sand to fight fires during the fire-bombing of Hamburg in 1943—the firebombing that had made an island of my mother's home and likely led to her PTSD.

We met up later that evening and I shepherded the group back to the memory-laden *Ratsweinkeller*. We were in high spirits as we planned next day to partake in the Hamburg Harbour Festival celebrating the 819th birthday of the harbour. I marveled at the long traditions of which I was a part. "*Hummel Hummel*," you say? Well, "*mors, mors*!" I knew the password. I was a Hamburger![21]

Our group of seven took the subway to get to the crowded harbour the day after our *Ratsweinkeller* celebrations. Tall ships, booths with bangles, pickles and beer, rides and musical groups drew thousands of celebrants to the river. It was difficult keeping our little international band together in the dense hordes, but we rounded out the day with a ferry ride up and down the Elbe. Perfect!

The Restaurant Arkadasch, meaning "friend" in Turkish, right across from the Jewish community centre was perfect for the large group supper that evening. No one but I knew that it was but a few doors from Bornstrasse 8, a Jewish house from which Hamburg's dispossessed Jews were sent to their deaths. Even without the knowledge of Bornstrasse, the fate of the Jews in Hamburg hung heavily in the air until we had a few drinks and relaxed into what we are there to do, to celebrate someone who had made it back from the brink of annihilation, my Oma, Anna Skrainka Schilling.

My walk brought her back among us and I knew Oma was pleased with the company at the Arkadasch: her granddaughter

---

21 The call "Hummel, Hummel!" refers to a water carrier who lived in Hamburg from 1787 to 1854. When children teased him, Hummel would answer, "mors, mors", roughly translated to, "kiss my ass!" The call is now used affectionately to identify Hamburgers.

and David, whom she had met in Canada; her nephew from Venezuela via Spain; Thomas, the son of one of the relatives who had been kind to her daughter during WWII and his wife Sylvie-lyn whom she had met several times; Renate, a member of parliament in Rhine-Westphalia with her husband Ludwig an arts connoisseur and two German filmmakers, Paul and Gerlinde Schwartz. It was a wonderful, warm and intelligent group.

Sometime in the evening, there was a toast, which Oma took with a smile, that is, the Oma in me. We told a few walk stories, but mainly, we just enjoyed the food and friendship. We sat at the Arkadasch at Grindelhof 17 on a fault line to the past, but we were very much in the present. Oma's and my journeys had cast light on stories that needed to be told, and reconciliations that needed to be made. I was happy to be a part of this group.

We saw the Hendricks and Schwartzes for one last breakfast and then had a few days with Sylvie-lyn, Thomas and Jorge. Sylvie-lyn outdid herself with dinners, which she served in their wonderfully groomed backyard. I had been on the road for over a month, blessed with extraordinary support from friends and relatives. How could I leave it behind?

David left first. He drove to Prague to return Robbie's car. I would head back to Canada on my own. It was a sad departure as David programmed the GPS and loaded the car. I had never felt closer to him in all our years of marriage. For three weeks he had been relaxed, patient, supportive and funny.

Finally, I was on my own, waiting for my flight to Canada. I knew I still had one task. I had to work through the feelings I had towards my mother. I had let her negative voice influence me and I heard it still. Wartime had made her hate Germany, deny her Jewish roots and mistrust everyone. She was an angry person. She had tried to get me to follow in her footsteps of hate, mistrust and denial. I chose to walk in Oma's footsteps.

Oma had been traumatized by war, but she had found solace in music and had trusted people enough to remarry when she was 56-years-old. My mother suffered badly from the effects of post-traumatic stress disorder all her life. I finally understood that.

I also understood that thanks to Intergenerational trauma I had been a challenge. I ran away at least twice as a child; I exhibited the usual teenage rebellion and serious illnesses had made parenting me difficult. It didn't matter what had caused my behaviours and illnesses because the end result was that I was difficult. My mother and I had not reconciled in life because we had not understood our actions in terms of trauma and its transmission. We had let anger shut down true bonding and failed to connect through our strengths—and we both had many.

The perfidy of Adolf Hitler and the Nazi party led to death and devastation of far too many individuals. But, the human toll of that era in terms of trauma and Intergenerational trauma resounds to this day. It will go on. It requires understanding and compassion to forgive and to move on.

As I sat by myself on my single bed in my room at Baseler Hof, I came to know with certainty that I had to forgive my mother—she whom I had refused to hug after ten-years-of-age. I had in a way forgiven her in a story I'd written about a Nazi perpetrator named Harlander whose path had unknowingly crossed my mother's and mine in Whitby, our Canadian hometown. I wrote:

> *I wish to make this apology to my mother now years after her death. Not fully understanding the betrayals she lived and the horrors she saw, I belittled her concerns and, dismissed them as paranoia. I know that we mostly live among good people. Life has taught me that. But, evil took shape for my mother. It was in the form of German betrayers and murderers whom she felt always around her. It went by the name of Harlander in my home town. It can take shape again. We need to listen to those who have seen evil.*

My mother lashed out at those she loved because she was shaped by wider forces. It was not my misaligned shoes in the hallway and not my refusal to drive her to an appointment that led to the curse, "I wish you had never been born!"

It was with that understanding that I finally called my mother to come to me in a room like the ones we had shared at Baseler Hof. It took a while, but she, who had been long dead, took shape before me. I saw her beautiful face as through the diaphanous curtains she'd brought with her from Germany to Canada. They fluttered open and in a split second of clarity, I looked into my mother's blue eyes and with an open heart, I forgave her. I hope that when I die, she will do the same—that we will talk and love, as we should.

I attribute the incomprehensible resilience I had as a child to my Jewish ancestors.

I marveled that I had spent 40 days in the wilderness to come to this point. But, therein lay the secret of walking with Oma. I had needed the time out of time to set myself on the path to understanding. I was ready to go home.

A few days later I boarded the plane back to Toronto. As we were about to take off, I spotted the first of them, the little figures. They were floating above the heads of the passengers. The small shifting forms, dressed mostly in black and grey antiquated garb, bounced around like excited children in the airplane's upper cabin. Among their thick accents I hear one say, "If de Maedele can come to us, den sure, we go wid her."

The signs said, "Buckle seatbelts." Not this lot. One, quite shrunken in size, perched audaciously on my shoulder. He shouted back at the others tumbling in the air. At take-off they were strung together like a streamer on an electric fan, laughing uproariously. My goodness, I thought. They've come to join me—my Jewish ancestors! Although they were unruly in their enthusiasm, I was delighted. My Jewish ancestors were coming with me to Canada! I settled in for the ride home, content, because in death, even in mass death dealt out by tyrants, there is no dominion. It had been a wonderful journey.

As I drifted off I saw Oma through a verdigris haze. She was waiting for me, smiling.

Afterword and Acknowledgments

Anna Skrainka Schilling, 1899-1976, married musician Franz Haertge in 1956. It was a happy marriage that lasted to Haertge's death in 1968. For simplicity, I omitted this husband with whom she daily played music. My mother, Suse Schilling, 1923-2000, married Frank Eggert, after the *Nuremberg Laws* ceased to have their discriminatory effect. The beginnings of life in Canada were rough but Frank and Suse worked determinedly to succeed and to contribute to Canadian society—which they did. My parents were founding members of the art gallery in Oshawa, part of the group that established the Whitby Art Gallery and they donated (through myself and my brother) the Fick-Eggert Collection of German Art to the Art Gallery of Ontario. My mother was president of the Victoria Women's Association for a few years and Eggert Court in Whitby is named after my parents for their environmental advocacy.

The walk in the Elbe River Valley took place in 2008 and as a result persons in the story are deceased. Robbie Lavack died in 2019, just short of his 99th birthday. His kind wife Ingela Lavack does not appear in the story for the sake of narrative economy. I thank Ingela for her frequent hospitality. Helga and Horst Gaebler, Marlene Kleinhans, Vera Wildgruber and Gerlinde Schwartz have died. I lost touch with other period witnesses and charming drivers but I value their contributions to this story. Thomas and Sylvie-lyn Reif, Ludwig and Renate Hendricks, Jorge Skrainka, Paul Schwartz, Constanze Hauf, Siegfried Tauch and Leonore Thielemann are doing well and I thank them for their support, past and present. Many Czech individuals assisted me: Daniela Srbova and her son Ondrej Srba, Lucie Ondrackova and Karel Malina. Ivona Pokorna of the Swedish Embassy in

Prague and her former colleague, Martina Storek, helped with translations and contacts. Douglas Skrainka of St Louis, Missouri, shared the extensive Skrainka research done by Mary Ryan of California in the 1980s. This was pivotal. John Freund, a Theresienstadt and Birkenau survivor fostered the search for my Jewish ancestors. Amanda K. Hale, Janet Kirkconnell, Lucy E. Black, Beverley Freedman, Ariane Blackman and Anita Eckhaus inspired changes in the text, but, more importantly, supported it with great kindness. I am especially indebted to Lucy who put the mirror of Intergenerational trauma before my eyes and then devoted herself to the necessary changes to reflect it in my story.

Mary Cook's design work for the cover, my website and for promotional materials has been superb, as always. It is always a pleasure working with her. I have come to know Chris Needham of NON more recently, but my thanks to Now Or Never could not be more heartfelt. The road to publication has been long and that makes me appreciate Chris and the NON team even more.

I am also deeply appreciative of Judy Stonkus who saw me around Lake Ontario and along the Elbe River. And, could acknowledgements fail to appreciate the family? No! I could not image my voyage through life without David, our daughter Jennifer and our granddaughters Charlotte and Samantha. I especially love David's patience with me. The experiences of the Elbe River Valley were 600 kilometres and six decades in the making. I hope my rendering provides a shortcut for others. We all need to walk comfortably with our past.

Discussion questions for book clubs, secondary schools, and for thinking about *Walking with Oma*—loosely based on Bloom's Taxonomy

A. Knowledge

1. Who are four of the main characters in the story?
2. In which countries, cities and towns does the story take place?
3. Where does the story end?
4. What is intergenerational trauma?
5. Briefly describe one period witness's story.

B. Comprehension

1. Who are the period witnesses and why are they called that?
2. How were Oma and her daughter Suse classified differently under the *Nuremberg Laws*?
3. Why does Suse reject her Jewish heritage and her daughter, the author, seek it out?
4. What realizations/understanding does the author come to while she walks?
5. Who is Robbie Lavack and how does he tie into the story?

C. Application

1. Give an example of a period witness in your own life and tell a little bit about his/her story. What time period does your period witness represent?
2. Provide an example of one intergenerational trauma story you heard or read about. What did you learn from it?
3. How does anything in the author's story relate to you or to persons you know?
4. If Germans as a whole are guilty of the atrocities of the Hitler era, are Canadians as a whole guilty of the First Nations residential school issues?
5. To which character in *Walking with Oma* do you relate and why?

D. Analysis

1. The author carries several story lines, that of her growing understanding about her own past, her experiences walking in Germany, and that of the stories of her mother, Oma and period witness stories from the past. Which story line is strongest and why?
2. Does the author really forgive her mother? Should she have blamed her to begin with?
3. Can German war guilt or the guilt about First Nations mistreatment be erased? How should they be dealt with?
4. How do the drivers who advance the walkers' luggage add to the themes of the story? And what are some of the other themes?
5. The author, her mother and her Oma experience trauma and intergenerational trauma in different ways. Can their experiences be compared?

E. Synthesis

1. Pass around one piece of paper. Each person writes a one word reaction to the book, folds the paper and passes it to the next person. Open the folded paper, read out the words and discuss the different reactions.
2. Tell one anecdote about a realization you made while walking a longer distance.
3. If you were to make a movie of the book, who would you cast as the author, her mother and Oma? Explain your choices.
4. Ten-second responses. The group leader calls out a topic and each person has ten seconds to list a response. After a series of ten-second responses, circle three that you liked best and report on them to the group. Topics: walking, Germany, Holocaust, memories of childhood, guilt, reconciliation, grandmother, WWII.
5. If you had to tell one other person what you learned from reading *Walking with Oma,* what would it be?

5. Evaluation

1. Who is the best target audience for *Walking with Oma* and why?
2. Is the story too sympathetic towards Germans or period witnesses? If so, how would you correct that?

3. Conflicted identity is common to Canadian immigrants. What other books deal with conflicted identity and how do they compare to or contrast with *Walking with Oma*?
4. What would you have liked to have seen footnoted or further explained and why?
5. Give *Walking with Oma* one to five stars and explain why in a single sentence.